KARMA

Cover art by

Jane A. Evans

KARMA
The Universal Law of Harmony

Edited by
VIRGINIA HANSON and ROSEMARIE STEWART

This publication made possible with the assistance of the Kern Foundation

The Theosophical Publishing House
Wheaton, Ill. U.S.A.
Madras, India/London, England

This is a Quest book, published by the Theosophical Publishing House, a department of the Theosophical Society in America.

Library of Congress Cataloging in Publication Data

Karma, the universal law of harmony

"A Quest book."
Includes bibliographical references.
1. Karma—Addresses, essays, lectures.
I. Hanson, Virginia. II. Stewart, Rosemarie,
1925-
BP573.K3K37 1981 291.2'2 80-53951
ISBN 0-8356-0543-4 (pbk.)

Printed in the United States of America

CONTENTS

CONTENTS

FOREWORD

Action is as natural to man as breathing. To breathe, ultimately, is to act, for the very pulsation of the breath displaces atoms in space, releases energies, and disturbs or reestablishes equilibrium. Breathing but mirrors the universal ebb and flow of all cyclic processes, and in the act of breathing we affirm our connection with the uiversal. The rhythm of inbreathing and outbreathing — inhalation and exhalation — should give us a clue to all action: whatever goes out must eventually turn upon itself for a return journey inwards; whatever moves within must one day be given *ex*pression.

Man has always pondered the nature of his action, seeking either to escape the consequences of his acts or to modify the results in such a manner as to insure no harm will come to him. To accept full responsibility for all our choices, and hence for all our actions, requires often more courage than we possess and maturity we long to achieve yet seemingly cannot attain. Only when the outcome of our choices is happy do we claim credit for right action; when the consequence is painful, we are quick to deny any association with the causative factors, attributing the outcome to circumstances or our genetic structure.

Choice — self-conscious choice — is a specifically human capability; to abrovate our right to choose between alternatives, even the right to say no to all choices, is to forfeit some part of our humanity. To permit others to make our choices for us is in itself a choice, and we must still pay the price demanded by the consequences of our default. Every moment of every day presents us with innumerable choices: what we shall think, what we shall feel, what we shall do. At times it may appear we are chosen by our thoughts or emotions, but this is only because we have permitted the mind or the heart to move without conscious direction, a choice which can be reversed whenever we decide to determine consciously what thoughts will occupy the mind or what feelings will be harbored in the heart.

Out of our choices, then, arises the complex pattern of our existence, each choice weaving the invisible web of circumstances in which we find ourselves enmeshed. Inherent in every action is the burden of its consequence, for action and reaction are ever polarized in life itself. All the great religious traditions have recognized this basic polarity. For the Buddhist, the recurrent cycles of birth and death are subject to the law of interdependent origination, recognizing that the wheel is turned by man's own hand; for the Hindu, the inexorable law of *karma,* action which ever turns upon itself in reaction, operates throughout the universe; for the Christian, the assurance that "whatsoever ye sow that shall ye also reap" is affirmation of a lawfulness pervading all universal processes. Throughout all nature, the interconnectedness of life in its manifold forms is evidenced, a universal law of harmony revealing itself again and again in innumerable patterns. If our own lives seem exempt from the harmonic law, it is but a lack of adequate perspective from which to view events. We may be too close in time or too near in space to observe with any accuracy or understanding the outcome of our choices, but to say law is not operative or pattern is not to be found is to fail to perceive the larger truth that order could not be anywhere were it not everywhere, harmony could not be achieved were lawfulness a sometime thing.

Action, of course, is more than physical movement; it is emotion and thought as well. The lawfulness of consequence, therefore is as much a moral principle as it is applicable to the physical realm of existence. The complexity of the web we weave is thereby enhanced, for motive, strength of thought or feeling, intentionality, all play their part in creating the outcome of any event or act. Karma, as the universal law that equilibrizes and harmonizes action and reaction, is not a "tit-for-tat" game; it is the universal dynamic constantly operative at every level, interweaving motive and act, intent and desire, motion and emotion. Ever adjusting, the law is both purposeful and merciful, for it is not the law which rewards or punishes, but we who by our choices bear both the joys and sorrows of those choices, weaving the patterns of our cyclic progress from nescience to omniscience as we mount the ladder of consciousness in the unfoldment of our divine potential.

FORWORD

One of the major contributions of The Theosophical Society has been the reintroduction into the western world of the long neglected and often forgotten concept of cyclic progression in accordance with universal law. The Sanskrit term, *karma*, has been adopted in English dictionaries as the all-embracing term for that universal law, the harmonic law of adjustment of compensation, action-reaction, to which all natural processes are subject. The ramifications of the law must be as endless and complex as those processes; yet in its ultimate simplicity, the law is harmony, the perfect relationship which obtains between all things everywhere. And as relationship, the law, finally, is known as love, the one true and abiding relationship in the universe.

In the essays that follow, comprising in this brief volume a survey of the meaning and nature of karma, various aspects of the universal law, the harmonics of love in action throughout the universe, are touched upon. But, as the Pseudo-Dionysius put it: "Man must not only learn the truth; he must suffer it." So our very lives give evidence of the patterns of the law, if we could but see, and when we learn to weave all patterns with the light of love, the fabric of existence will be luminous and our every act reflect the harmony of the divine.

— Joy Mills
FOREWORD

1.

THE CHRISTENING OF KARMA

Geddes MacGregor

The concept of karma, even when properly understood as specifying a universal moral principle that entails profound individual responsibility for one's actions, generally alarms Christians. That is partly because for various complex reasons reincarnationism has had a bad press in the history of Christian thought and practice. Despite the enormous body of literature in which it has appeared in the West, it still seems to many an alien and essentially Indian notion, as ill-fitted to a Christian outlook as would be a stupa or pagoda atop a Gothic church. Apart, however, from such widespread and perhaps not unnatural prejudices against the doctrine of karma and the reincarnationism with which it is associated (prejudices that are hardly worth considering here), some serious objections are raised by informed Christians to the proposal that the doctrine of karma may be with propriety christened as eminently reconcilable with Christian faith, even as that faith is interpreted by the most orthodox and traditionalist of Christians.

One of the most obvious of such objections is that Christian faith, being grounded in the recognition of the power of Jesus Christ to save me and, through his death and resurrection, to raise me (my sins notwithstanding) to everlasting life, can have no place for an inexorable moral law such as is implied in the concept of karma. This type of objection is likely to be raised more vehemently among those Christians who account themselves "Protestant" than among those who regard themselves as "Catholics". That this should be so looks at first somewhat paradoxical to those of us who recall that Kant, who has been traditionally revered in Protestant thought and feared by traditionalist Catholic thinkers, argues in the *Critique of Practical Reason* for a view that is almost an exact occidental counterpart of the oriental doctrine of karma. His "categorical imperative" expresses in encapsulated form the basic moral principle at the heart of the universe: duty. Not only is the universe subject to "physical laws" (the law of "the starry heavens above"); it is governed no less inexorably by another law, "the moral law within." This law, according to Kant, operates just as surely as the law of gravity or any other of the so-called "laws of physics." It is I alone, moreover, who am responsible for my actions, as are you for yours. If Kant's ethical teachings could be, as they have been, so palatable to Protestant Christian thought and so acceptable even to Catholic thought (for Catholic objection to his thought was not directed to his ethics but, rather, to his metaphysical skepticism), why should the notion of karma strike such terror in so many Christian hearts?

But let us probe deeper and into canonical Christian Scripture itself. In the Sermon on the Mount, that most venerated collection of the utterances of Jesus, these words are attributed to the Lord himself: "Do not imagine that I have come to abolish the Law or the Prophets. I have come not to abolish but to complete them. I tell you solemnly, till heaven and earth disappear, not one dot, not one little stroke, shall disappear from the Law until its purpose is achieved." (Matthew 5.17f Jerusalem Bible) Jesus is speaking, of course, of the Torah — to Jews still the most sacred part of the Bible. He is saying that the *formulations* of the moral law that is at the heart of all things may be inadequate and so may be improved or enriched; but the Law itself is unchangeable. It is, as the psalmist had said long before, "perfect, new life for the soul." (Psalm 19.7 Jerusalem Bible) So Jesus goes on: "Therefore, the man who infringes even one of the least of these commandments and teaches others to do the same will be considered the least in the kingdom of heaven; but the man who keeps them and teaches them will be considered great in the kingdom of heaven. For I tell you, if your virtue goes no deeper than that of the scribes and Pharisees, you will never get into the kingdom of heaven." (Matthew 19f Jerusalem Bible) These words, from him whom Christians acknowledge as Lord and acclaim as Savior and Redeemer, leave one in no doubt that no Christian dare pretend to a means of by-passing the moral law which Jesus describes in almost exactly the terms in which one would describe the law of karma.

The karmic law does not exclude grace and redemption any more than does the Torah to which Jesus was referring. Paul rejoices, as must all Christians, that grace has come through Jesus Christ; but he deplores those (and no doubt there were many then as there are today) who proposed to ignore the Law and let grace take over and replace it, making the Law redundant. "Does it follow that we should remain in sin so as to let grace have greater scope?" he asks rhetorically and immediately answers his own question: "Of course not." (Romans 6.1. Jerusalem Bible) Grace gives me a unique opportunity; it puts me in a privileged position by providing conditions of unheard-of advantage; but it no more erases the Law than my good fortune in having a good teacher absolve me from the need to learn. A good teacher helps me to learn. He or she may even make my education possible where otherwise it would have been, for all practical purposes, a hopeless enterprise. So Christianity can take the karmic law with all its entailments under its wing as, following its Master's precept, it must take the Torah.

Why, then, is there so much resistance to the concept of karma and its entailments on the part of those who look to Jesus as Savior and Lord? It is not easy to avoid the conclusion that antinomianism (the view that Christians are by grace freed from the need to obey the Law or even to recognize it) is, under various guises and sometimes ingenious disguises, more widespread in the Christian Church than is commonly supposed either within it or outside it. A genuinely deep concern for morality and righteousness cannot be said to be strikingly characteristic either of the leaders of the Church or of the average churchgoer. A passion for justice is certainly no more characteristic of the assemblies of the Church than is a passionate concern for the truth, the absence of which was cited by Lord Russell as his fundamental reason for not being a Christian. Yet every educated Christian must surely know that no talk of grace without the Law is like talking of literature without language. Indeed, it is much worse: it is like talking of love without sacrifice.

What, according to Christian teaching, does Christ do for the Christian? What is the nature of his redemptive work? The answer, however formulated, is essentially this: he puts the Christian in the right way, providing the conditions that make possible his or her salvation. Through faith in Christ the Christian is "justified," that is, "put right," so that it is now possible for him or for her, as before it was not, to be "sanctified," that is, to get out of the bind and make progress in spiritual development. It is the discovery of the aid that Christ provides in this undertaking that causes the Christian to be, in C. S. Lewis's felicitous phrase, "surprised by joy."

More serious is the theological objection that, while a program of spiritual evolution attained through reincarnation, may be thinkable for Christian believers, it cannot apply to Christ himself who, according to Christian orthodoxy, is "fully God" and "fully man." Since he is God, how can he (as God is conceived in the biblical, Judaeo-Christian tradition) need to progress anywhere at all? Yet if he is also, as Church doctrine insists, "fully man," how can he *not* need to progress, since this is the nature of humanity, according to orthodox Christian doctrine, must be preserved: to do injury to the one is as bad as to do injury to the other. Such reflections lead us to a more profound one still. When the early Christians acknowledged Jesus Christ as Lord and Savior of the world, what precisely did they mean? Not only were they far from thinking in terms of possibly inhabited planets on solar systems in distant galaxies, as surely we must think today; their knowledge of planet Earth itself was very limited. Their world extended little beyond the Mediterranean basin.

May not it be that other planets in the trillions of galaxies in the universe have their own counterparts to Jesus Christ, their own unique incarnations of God? A Savior who is "True God and True Man" is fitting indeed for "us men and for our salvation," as the Christian creed has it; but suppose there are Martians on Mars. He would not be fitting for them. They would presumably need a Savior who is True God and True Martian. So then, since we are being for the moment so speculative, suppose that we have just had a radio signal from a planet in some distant galaxy. We should all be very excited, of course. Christians would be eager to know whether the inhabitants had heard of Jesus Christ. Suppose that they had not but that they had had on their own planet a Being who was the focus of one of their major religions and seemed to function in it precisely the way in which Jesus Christ functions in orthodox Christianity. Would a Christian then be justified in saying, in effect: "No, no, that will not do at all. We must collect money and see that messages are transmitted at once to the other planet to bring them the Good News that the True Savior, the unique Son of God, chose this planet Earth, and that they must therefore acquaint themselves without delay with him and his teaching and accept him as their Savior?" Would a Christian then also feel bound in conscience, the first time that a spaceship went to the other planet, to see that included in the passenger list was a team of missionaries armed with a large supply of Bibles duly translated into whatever language was appropriate to the planetary needs of the new missionary field? Would that spaceship cross one coming in the other direction with emissaries from the other planet addressed to the Patriarch of Constantinople, the Archbishop of Canterbury, the Pope, and the President of the World Council of Churches, in hope of converting their faithful to an allegiance to *their* Savior and Lord?

If that seems absurd, as surely many will perceive it to be, a way is open for the orthodox Christian to say, in effect: "I cannot tell what has been the pilgrimage of Jesus Christ before his incarnation on this planet of ours, nor can I dare to prognosticate what his future role on other planets may be. I cannot see, however, why he should not be part of an evolutionary process too, although his stage in the process is infinitely beyond the one in which, by his grace, I am mercifully making some little progress here and now." So not even this objection need have the weight it seems to many Christians to carry.

The next objection to the reincarnational implicates of the karmic law that I should like to consider here is partly philosophical, partly theological. According to reincarnational teaching, the Self transcends in some way the personalities into which it is periodically incarnated. We know, however, that the brain functions as a computer and that this computer not only deteriorates with age but can be irreparably injured by an automobile accident or other traumatic experience in such a way as to destroy memory. The claims of reincarnationists notwithstanding, it is plain that most people remember nothing of a previous life and if what has just been noticed about the functioning of the brain be true, that is unsurprising. For many Christians the notion of a "subtle body" or "etheric double" or "store of energy" to carry over from one incarnation to another the memory-function seems fanciful, no less than does Plato's symbol of the waters of Lethe through which souls pass on their way to the next incarnation, so that all but a few indomitable and advanced souls who manage to keep their heads just a little above these waters of forgetfulness are completely deprived of the power to remember anything of an alleged past life.

This is, of course, a standard and serious philosophical objection (however answerable it may seem) to reincarnationism in general. We should notice, however, that what applies to the reincarnational goose applies no less to the Christian gander. Central to all Christian orthodoxy and the supreme focus of the *kerygma* or proclamation of the first apostles of Christianity is the doctrine of Resurrection. Because Jesus Christ has been "raised from the dead," those who acknowledge and receive him will rise too; that is, they will die but eventually receive a new body. Paul calls it a "glorious" body, one that is presumably finer and better, more ductile and of greater luminosity than our present one. But now, suppose that I have died and have been invested with this new and glorious body of which Paul so eloquently writes. Surely I must be filled with gratitude for what Christ did for me to make all this possible; yet how can I be able to have such thankfulness if I cannot remember my life in the physical body, the life in which my salvation was begun? And how can I remember anything about this life by means of my "glorified" brain or whatever instrument is its counterpart in the luminous body I have now been accorded? In short, whatever difficulties attend reincarnationist doctrine apply in exactly the same way to the indubitably orthodox Christian doctrine of the resurrection of the body.

Christians, especially those with a Catholic background, also often feel that the karmic principle and its reincarnational implicates encourage an individualist approach to such an extent as not only to remove the need for the Church, its ministry, and its sacraments which the Church deems necessary for salvation, but also to eliminate all need of guidance and help. True, reincarnationism, grounded in the karmic principle, does make a "lone walk" possible. It does abolish the need to depend absolutely on the Church's ministry and sacraments. That is not to say, however, that any sane man or woman, Christian or otherwise, would fail to use any help he or she can find in so momentous an enterprise as one's salvation. The fact that I can, if I am reasonably intelligent, educate myself entirely from books does not imply that I shall on that account decline the services of good teachers. On the contrary, the more intelligent I am the more readily shall I see their value to me. Nevertheless, *in extremis* I can do without a teacher and fend for myself. If it should happen that I can find only very bad teachers I may well prefer to manage on my own, for a bad teacher may be even worse than none. He may impede an intelligent person's progress. So a stupid priest or ignorant rabbi or lazy guru could be an impediment that I might well be better without.

A thorough knowledge of the history of the Christian Church leaves us in little doubt that much of the prejudice against karmic and reincarnationist teaching has been generated by the fears of those bad bishops and pedestrian priests who, having no spirituality of their own to offer, perceive the danger that such spiritual independence poses to their power over the lives of men and women. Good priests, however, have nothing to fear and indeed everything to welcome from the development of spiritual independence among the faithful. In fact, many of the greatest Christians, those who plainly have been conspicuously able to fend for themselves in their spiritual development have been no less conspicuously ready to learn from any teacher or confessor or friend and also to participate in the life of the Church with the simplest of "babes" in the faith. One thinks, for instance, of Teresa of Avila, of George Tyrrell, of Kierkegaard, of Simone Weil, to mention only a random few. They have deeply loved the Church without finding it absolutely indispensable. I very much love my home without deeming it absolutely essential to life and happiness.

The suspicion, voiced long ago by A. E. Taylor in *The Faith of a Moralist,* that reincarnationism encourages procrastination also warrants notice. Of course one can put off reform to another life, but one knows all the while that one is only making things more difficult for oneself. Most people manage to procrastinate copiously even with no expectation of the "second chance" that reincarnationism provides. Augustine's youthful prayer, "Give me chastity but not yet," is as possible without a karmic view as with one. The deathbed-repentance syndrome is familiar to all pastors and confessors. The moral urgency implied in either a reincarnationist or a non-reincarnationist view is always there. The sooner I reform, the easier my reformation will be; the longer I delay, the more trouble I make for myself. Every drunk learns that.

Some Christians object that reincarnationism is inconsistent with the Christian teaching that our destiny is settled once for all at death. There is, however, no such clear Christian teaching. Indeed, the Christian teaching on the afterlife is, for various reasons, by far the most confused part of traditional theology. It is so for some very good reasons, one of which is that in the first century of the Christian Way people did not give it much thought because they expected the end of the world imminently, perhaps literally on the morrow. In such circumstances one does not readily engage in eschatological speculations. When eventually that expectation died down, churchmen were confronted with a vast panorama of possibilities from both their Hebrew heritage and their Hellenistic surroundings. The most promising line of early Christian thought was that which pointed to a state of purgation and growth, a notion which, found in Clement of Alexandria and others among the early Fathers, was later developed in singularly unfortunate ways in the Latin West as the medieval doctrine of purgatory. Along with this doctrine of an "intermediate state," however, were developed the notions of heaven and hell, states generally presented as unchanging conditions, the one of eternal bliss, the other of eternal torment. Such notions are infact unthinkable not only because the doctrine of hell is incmpatible with the doctrine of God's love and mercy, but because both heaven and hell exclude growth, which is of the very nature of all finite being. Most educated Christians have quietly set aside the notions of heaven and hell in the form in which they were presented in the Middle Ages and by the Reformation Fathers.

The objection that it is immoral to be held accountable for sins one has committed in a previous life and has therefore forgotten deserves some attention, since at first sight it seems plausible. How can I have the disposition of penitence for my misdeeds if I cannot even remember them? We may well argue that if a child is to be punished the punishment should be swift, since otherwise the child will soon have forgotten the wrong it did and therefore rightly resent the punishment. But while that may be sound parental practice for the training of the very young, life operates on different lines. Modern psychoanalysis recognizes that what gives us most trouble is what lies buried in our unconscious. It is our forgotten misdeeds and evil thoughts that take the worst toll. Christian theology abundantly recognizes the fact that we do not know how distorted we are. Like it or not, we do have to pay the price for past wrongdoing we have we have forgotten about. It is so easy to injure my brother and then forget about it. The greater the injury the more ready I am to forget, that is, to push the memory of it down into my unconscious. There, however, it continues to fester. The reincarnationist, grounded as he is in the karmic principle, is only extending the scene, knowing as he does that man has a much longer history than the date on his birth certificate. He has also a longer future than the date that is to be on his death certificate: a future he can make or mar.

Many Christians believe in a literalistic way in the Second Coming of Christ as a "day," the *dies irae,* the Day of Judgment. Is not that alien to a reincarnationist view? It may be incompatible with some forms of reincarnationism, but not all. We can still interpret the Day of Judgment as the end of the present age and the beginning of a new one, which is indeed in accord with the biblical witness. The new age, if this planet Earth be destroyed, might begin on another planet in another galaxy, if not on one in our own. The holocaust that many Christians envision on that "terrible day" would presumably in any case wipe out all life, including the vast animal kingdom to which we are biologically related through evolution: a relationship to which, by the way, Christian theologians have never given adequate attention, despite the poetry of Francis of Assisi and the Gospel assurance that God notes the fall of the smallest sparrow to the ground.

The Cambridge moralist, A. C. Ewing, in a sympathetic but critical reference to reincarnationism and the karmic principle, suggested that it has too much of a "mercantile flavor," too much of "an exact proportion between such incommensurables as goodness and happiness." In such a scenario, he suggests, there could be no genuine self-sacrifice. True, Christian love knows nothing of moral accountancy. Christ, far from calculating the cost of our redemption, pours forth his blood for us on the Cross with infinite abandon. The cost of our redemption, however, may be even greater than Ewing perceived. Thomas Aquinas, preeminent among the medieval schoolmen, taught that grace presupposes nature and perfects it. If then, God, in his self-humbling, must reckon with both law and nature, the cost of sacrificial love must surely be incalculably higher than we can imagine. The karmic principle abides.

What the karmic principle and its reincarnational implicates do provide is a mitigation of, if not a complete solution to, the most intractable problem in Christian theology: the problem of evil. They spread the story of the individual on to a much larger canvas, so that in looking at our present life we are looking at only a slice (indeed a very slim slice) of the moving picture that stretches far into the future as well as deeply into the past.

Long before anyone knew of outer galaxies or could have thought seriously about the possibility of interplanetary travel, Alice Meynell (1847-1922), a profoundly mystical English Catholic poet, hinted in a poem at the problem that the magnitude of the universe posed for Christology even in her time. Entitled *Christ in the Universe,* it contains allusions such as these:

No planet knows that this
Our wayside planet, carrying land and wave,
Love and life multiplied, and pain and bliss,
Bears as chief treasure one forsaken grave.

Nor, in our little day,
May his devices with the heavens be guessed;
His pilgrimage to thread the Milky Way,
Or His bestowals there be manifest.

But in the eternities
Doubtless we shall compare together, hear
A million alien gospels, in what guise
He trod the Pleiades, the Lyre, the Bear.[1]

O, be prepared, my soul!
To read the inconceivable, to scan
The myriad forms of God those stars unroll
When, in our turn we show to them a Man.

Perhaps, however, nothing so much impedes the christening of karma as does an objection and misunderstanding that we considered near the outset: the notion that emphasizing individual responsibility for salvation undercuts the operation of Christ's redemptive act. Since this is probably the most popular misconception on the subject, especially among Protestant Christians, I wish to make abundantly clear to readers of this essay, Christian or otherwise, that this objection arises more

[1]*The Golden Book of Modern English Poetry,* 1870-1920 (London and Toronto: Dent and Sons, 1927), p. 51.

from a misunderstanding of Christian doctrine than from a misunderstanding of the karmic principle itself.

The notion that, when one is captured by the power of Christ's love and responds in fervent gratitude for the salvation he assures the recipient of his grace, that is the end of the matter, is not a Christian notion at all. It is a pernicious travesty of Christian doctrine as taught in the New Testament, the early Fathers, and not least the Reformation Fathers. A tradition that runs all the way from Paul through Augustine to Luther and Calvin demands that Christians be especially on their guard against the notion that when one has become aware of the saving act of Christ in the soul there is nothing more to be done.

I have elsewhere told the story of a stuttering Christian missionary who, on being taunted that Christ did not seem to have healed him, replied: "But b-b-before he h-h-healed me I was a d-d-deaf-m-m-mute." Until his conversion his condition had been hopeless; now it was remediable. There is also an old Victorian poem about a little girl who, having covered her school "slate" with figures in trying to solve an arithmetic problem, comes weeping to the teacher who, being a good and kind teacher, sits down beside the child, cleans the slate and says, "Now let us do it together." The teacher's action becomes, in the poem, a parable of the work of salvation that Christ begins in the soul. Would such an action diminish the gratitude of such a child? Should such a recognition of the nature of Christ's saving love diminish a Christian's appreciation and gratitude? Of course not. If you had a mental block against mathematics that made math a fruitless pain to you, its removal would make doing math a pleasure; the last thing it would do for you would be to cause you to stop doing mathematics. If you were an alcoholic down and out in the gutter and then through Christ found your way to redemption from your vice and the path to a productive and creative life, the last thing you would do would be to insist that you had no longer any need to consider the tendency that had brought you so low in the first place. On the contrary, you would be all the more aware of it and at the same time aware of your power to overcome it, which you did not have before.

"So then, my dear friends," writes Paul to the Church at Philippi, "continue to do as I tell you, as you always have; not only as you did when I was there with you, but even more now that I am no longer there; and work for your salvation 'in fear and trembling.' It is God, for his own loving purposes, who puts both the will and the action into you." (Philippians 2.12f. Jerusalem Bible)

Is there, then, any sound theological reason from any Christian point of view, orthodox or heterodox, traditionalist or experimental, against the christening of karma and its reincarnational implicates? Personally I cannot see any at all. The influence on Christianity of Hellenistic ideas, including of course the Platonic tradition, was not merely something that developed after the apostles of the Christian Way had spread their message to the Gentile world; it was present, to say the least, in the Judaism in which the Christian Way was cradled. During what Christian scholars have customarily called the "intertestamental period" (that is, approximately 165 B.C. through A.D. 48, the interval between the last book of the Hebrew canon, Daniel, and the earliest of the New Testament writings), the Jews were exposed to vast extraneous influences. Jewish thought, even in Palestine, was profoundly affected by these. The kind of movement of which Jesus was the center, however we may choose to interpret it, would have been unthinkable in Palestine a few centuries earlier. By his time, however, the situation had so altered that Hellenistic ideas could be commingled with traditional Jewish faith and practice in a rabbi's teaching. In Alexandria, the chief intellectual center of the Diaspora, the Hellenistic influence was overwhelming, having a most able spokesman in Philo, a contemporary of Jesus; but even in the Jewish Homeland its effects, if less enduring, were considerable. Greek architectural ideas affected even the way in which synagogues were built and Greek administrative practices were adopted by Jewish communities in their government and organization. Hellenism was fostered, at least for a time, by the priestly aristocracy. While Jesus himself encouraged the veneration of the Torah and in principle honored the traditional Jewish ritual and other customs, his leadership of the kind of celibate religious community into which he organized his disciples was alien to classical Hebrew practice. The *extent* to which Hellenistic ideas affected his teaching is controversial; what is indisputable is that Hellenistic ideas had so permeated the thought of would be like suggesting that an educated American today could be ignorant of Darwin or of Freud or that he or she might not have heard of nuclear fission.

We all know that Plato, following the Pythagorean tradition, accepted the ancient doctrine of reincarnation, very explicitly putting it into the mouth of the Socrates of the Dialogues. Long before Christianity was in the way of being directly influenced by Platonistic and Neoplatonistic ideas in the pagan world, however, it had emerged in an atmosphere in which reincarnationist ideas such as Plato took as part of the ideological scenery were at least an ingredient. Christians of the first century could not but have imbibed such ideas and there is some evidence to show that they did not by any means necessarily repudiate them. Some seem to have found them congenial. In the Alexandrian tradition that developed, in which Clement and Origen played leading roles, the thought of Plato loomed very large indeed.

Why, then, did reincarnationist teaching get such a bad press in the Christian Church and come to be so much distrusted, not to say feared? Only a combination of circumstances that included the inchoate state of Christian eschatology and the second-century Church leaders' suspicion of Gnostic teaching, could have led to the ousting of a reincarnationist interpretation of the life of the world to come that was and is the Christian hope. I think this result has gravely impoverished the Church's official presentation of the nature of the afterlife. As we have seen, there is really not the slightest reason for the fear or the distrust.

Of course that is not to say that reincarnationism in every form in which it happens to appear is necessarily reconcilable with Christian faith or that the Church ought to welcome Gnosticism no matter in what guise it comes. In some forms it can lead to and indeed express a selfish unconcern for others that would be radically antithetical to the *agape* - that Paul exalts above all else in one of his most eloquent passages (I Corinthians 13) and that is universally acclaimed by Christians as of the very life of the Church. Any *such* reincarnationism would be, on that account alone, entirely out of court. Moreover, reincarnationist teaching is sometimes so closely tied to certain metaphysical presuppositions not easily if at all reconcilable to Christian faith that a Christian with any pretensions to loyalty to the central creeds of the Church would be rightly cautious in regard to such forms of it. Nevertheless, when all that is said, there is nothing in the notion itself and certainly nothing in the karmic principle that lies behind it (whatever name be given to that principle) that need give a Christian of even the strictest orthodox stance the slightest puase. On the contrary, the karmic principle and its reincarnationist implicates can be warmly embraced by any such Christian as a means of greatly illuminating his or her understanding of the nature of the life of the world to come, belief in which is solemnly affirmed in the final article of the Nicene Creed with no specifying or limiting details of any kind. Cardinal Mercier is among the distinguished Roman Catholics who have declared that reincarnationism has never really been officially or explicitly condemned by the Church. The bad press it received was partly through a sort of guilt by association with other ideas and partly because of the fears we have considered earlier.

To such Christians as are interested in the karmic principle and the concept of reincarnation, I would say: by all means diligently study it through theosophical or any other well-informed channels and, bearing in mind the considerations I have laid before you here, discover through critical thought and earnest prayer whether it might not greatly clarify your understanding of the Christian hope and illumine your vision of your own destiny in the life of the world to come.

GEDDES MacGREGOR, Docteur-es-lettres (*summa cum laude,* Sorbonne), D.Phil., D.D. (Oxford), LL.B. (Edinburgh), F.R.S.L., L.H.D. (*h.c.,* Hebrew Union), is Emeritus Distinguished Professor of Philosophy and former Dean of the Graduate School of Religion, University of Southern California. He came to the U.S. in 1949 as the first holder of the Rufus Jones Chair of Philosophy and Religion. Recipient of the California Literature Award (Gold Medal, non-fiction category), he is the author of 24 books, all monographs, including his well-known *Philosophical Issues in Religious Thought.* He has lectured widely in American and other universities, has travelled extensively in Asia and Europe, is a member of Mensa, and has preached in pulpits such as Westminster Abbey and St. Paul's, London. Two of his books have been published as Quest Books: *Gnosis* and *Reincarnation in Christianity.* In the press is another book of his: *Reincarnation as a Christian Hope* (London: Macmillan, 1981). An Anglican priest who was for six years Canon Theologian in his diocese, he is ecumenically well known for his independent thought and internationally respected among Christian scholars, having also given more than forty years of ordained service to the Church. He is listed in such works as WHO'S WHO IN AMERICA, WHO'S WHO IN EUROPE, and WHO'S WHO (London).

2.

KARMA — THE WOMB OF TIME

[A selection of quotations from the works of H. P. Blavatsky]
— Lina Psaltis, Compiler

Karma as generally understood in the Western world is a rather vague term coming from the Eastern religious meaning, usually, a simplistic, when not moronic, idea that one has "good things or bad things" happening to him. H. P. Blavatsky, when writing upon this subject in the late 19th century had this to say when asked how theosophical principles can be applied to everyday living:

> Let me briefly remind you what these principles are — universal Unity and Causation; Human Solidarity; the Law of Karma; re-incarnation. These are the four links of the golden chain which should bind humanity into one family, one universal Brotherhood.[1]

The following quotations selected from her works are an effort to help the student find his way through the maze of life as it exists within the womb of time. It is only within the boundaries of our own individual experiences in life that we can arrive at a satisfying sense of where in space and time we exist.

[The following definition as given in the *Theosophical Glossary* involves terms unfamiliar, perhaps, to many readers.

However, in order to cover as much ground as possible they have been left undefined. It is to be hoped that the interested student will find them intriguing enough that more study will follow.]*

Karma (Sk.). Physically, action: metaphysically, the Law of Retribution, the Law of cause and effect or Ethical Causation. Nemesis, only in one sense, that of bad Karma. It is the eleventh *Nidana* in the concatenation of causes and effects in orthodox Buddhism; yet it is the power that controls all things, the resultant of moral action, the metaphysical *Samskara,* or the moral effect of an act committed for the attainment of something which gratifies a personal desire. There is the Karma of merit and the Karma of demerit. Karma neither punishes nor rewards, it is simply *the one* Universal Law which guides unerringly, and, so to say, blindly, all other laws productive of certain effects along the grooves of their respective causations. When Buddhism teaches† that "Karma is that moral kernel (of any being) which alone survives death and continues in transmigration" or reincarnation, it simply means that there remains nought after each Personality but the causes produced by it; causes which are undying, i.e., which cannot be eliminated from the Universe until replaced by their legitimate effects, and wiped out by them, so to speak, and such causes — unless compensated during the life of the person who produced them with adequate effects, will follow the reincarnated Ego, and reach it in its subsequent reincarnation until a harmony between effects and causes is fully reestablished. No "personality" — a mere bundle of material atoms and of instinctual and mental characteristics — can of course continue, as such, in the world of pure Spirit. Only that which is immortal in its very nature and divine in its essence, namely, the Ego, can exist for ever. And it is that Ego which chooses the personality it will inform, after each Devachan, and which receives through these personalities the effects of the Karmic causes produced, it is therefore the Ego, that *self* which is the "mortal kernal" referred to and embodied karma, "which alone survives death."[2]

---

* *All bracketed words in the following material are those of the compiler.*

† Readers who have not encountered this in their study of Buddhism are referred to the teachings of the Mahayana School.

[Karma, conceptually, cannot be separated from the concept of *Dharma. Dharma* is translated many ways, such as: duty, righteousness, mercy, etc. From dharma and karma, we arrive at the earliest known concept, and that is rta. All of these terms evolved in the richness of the Indian mind from a period perhaps pre-Vedic, hence possibly before the third millenium B.C. These philosophic teaching regarding the moral nature of man and the universe can then be read knowing that more than 5000 years of deliberation, contempolation and experimentation are involved.]

> . . . The law of Karma is a moral law, and where no moral responsibility exists, there can be no application of the law of Karma; but the law of cause and effect applies to all departments of nature.[3]
>
> . . . Exoteric religions base their morality on the hope of reward and fear of punishment at the hands of an Omnipotent Ruler of the Universe by following the rules he has at his pleasure laid down for the obedience of his helpless subjects; in some cases, however, religions of later growth have made morality to depend on the sentiment of gratitude to that Ruler for benefits received.[4]
>
> . . . There is one eternal Law in nature, one that always tends to adjust contraries and to produce final harmony. It is owing to this law of spiritual development superseding the physical and purely intellectual, that mankind will become freed from its false gods, and find itself finally — SELF-REDEEMED.[5]
>
> Karma is a word of many meanings, and has a special term for almost every one of its aspects. It means, as a synonym of sin, the performance of some action for the attainment of an object of *worldly*, hence *selfish*, desire, which cannot fail to be hurtful to somebody else. Karma is action, the Cause; and Karma again is "the law of ethical causation;" the *effect* of an act produced egotistically, when the great law of harmony depends on altruism.[6]
>
> . . . it is only this doctrine, we say, that can explain to us the mysterious problem of Good and Evil, and reconcile man to the terrible and *apparent* injustice of life. Nothing but such certainty can quiet our revolted sense of justice. For, when one unacquainted with the noble doctrine looks around him, and

observes the inequalities of birth and fortune, of intellect and capacities; when one sees honour paid fools and profligates, on whom fortune has heaped her favours by mere privilege of birth, and their nearest neighbour, with all his intellect and noble virtues — farm more deserving in every way — perishing of want and for lack of sympathy; when one sees all this and has to turn away, helpless to relieve the undeserved suffering, one's ears ringing and heart aching . . . that blessed knowledge of Karma alone prevents him from cursing life and men . . . .[7]

[The reality of man's inner powers and energies has become inherent to the culture of Western man. This awareness entails many other elements, such as a terminology within which we can communicate. The following selection serves this purpose]:

. . . To understand the idea [of reincarnation and karma] well you have to first study the dual sets of "principles": the *spiritual,* or those which belong to the imperishable Ego; and the *material,* or those principles which make up the ever-changing bodies or the series of personalities of that Ego. Let us fix permanent these, and say that: —

I. *Atma,* the *"Higher Self,"* is neither your Spirit nor mine, but like sunlight shines on all. It is the universally diffused *"divine principle,"* and is inseparable from its one and absolute *Meta*-Spirit, as the sunbeam is inseparable from sunlight.

II. *Buddhi* (the spiritual soul) is only its vehicle. Neither each separately, nor the two collectively, are of any more use to the body of man, than sunlight and its beams are for a mass of granite buried in the earth, *unless the divine Duad is assimilated by, and reflected in,* some *consciousness.* Neither Atma nor Buddhi is ever reached by Karma, *its working agent* of Itself in one aspect, and the other is unconscious *on this plane. This consciousness or mind is,*

III. *Manas,** the derivation or product in a reflected form of *Ahamkara,* "the conception of I," or Egoship. It is, therefore, when inseparably united to the first two, called the spiritual Ego, and *Taijasi* (the radiant). This is the real Individuality, or the divine man. It is this Ego which —

* Mahat or the "Universal Mind" is the source of Manas. The latter is Mahat, i.e., mind, in man. Manas is also called *Kshetrajna,* "embodied Spirit."

having originally incarnated in the *senseless* human form animated by, but unconscious (since it had no consciousness) of, the presence in itself of the dual monad — made of that human-like form ***a real man***. It is that Ego, that "Causal Body," which overshadows every personality Karma forces it to incarnate into; and this Ego, which is held responsible for all the sins committed through, and in, every new body or personality — the evanescent masks which hide the true Individual through the long series of rebirths.

ENQ. But is this just? Why should this Ego receive punishment as the result of deeds which it has forgotten?

THEO. It has not forgotten them, it knows and remembers its misdeeds as well as you remember what you have done yesterday. Is it because the memory of that bundle of physical compounds called "body" does not recollect what its predecessor (the personality *that was*) did, that you imagine that the real Ego has forgotten them? As well say it is unjust that the new boots on the feet of a boy, who is flogged for stealing apples, should be punished for that which they know nothing of.

ENQ. But if it is punished in this life for the misdeeds committed in a previous one, then it is this Ego that ought to be rewarded also, whether here, or when disincarnated.

THEO. And so it is. If we do not admit of any punishment outside of this earth, it is because the only state the Spiritual Self knows of, hereafter, is that of unalloyed bliss.

ENQ. What do you mean?

THEO. Simply this: ***crimes and sins committed on a plane of objectivity and in a world of matter, cannot receive punishment in a world of pure subjectivity***. We believe in no hell or paradise as localities; in no objective hell-fires and worms that never die, nor in any Jerusalems with streets paved with sapphires and diamonds. What we believe in is a *postmortem state* or mental condition, such as we are in during a vivid dream. We believe in an immutable law of absolute Love, Justice, and Mercy. And believing in it, we say: "Whatever the sin and dire results of the original Karmic transgression of the now incarnated Egos no man (or the outer material and periodical form of the Spiritual Entity) can be held, with any degree of justice, responsible for the consequences of his birth. He does not ask to be born, nor can he choose the parents that will give him life. In every respect he is a victim to his environment, the child of circumstances over which he has no control; and if each of his transgressions were impartially investigated, there would be found nine out of every ten cases when he was the one sinned against, rather than the sinner. Life is at best a heartless play, a story sea to cross, and a heavy burden often too difficult to bear. The greatest philosophers have tried in vain to fathom and find out its *faison d'etre,* and have failed except those who had the key to it, namely, the Eastern sages. Life is, as Shakespeare describes it: —

> ". . . . but a walking shadow — a poor player,
> That struts and frets his hour upon the stage,
> And then is heard no more. It is a tale
> Told by an idiot, full of sound and fury,
> Signifying nothing . . . . "

Nothing in its separate part, yet of the greatest importance in its collectively or series of lives. At any rate, almost every individual life is, in its full development, a sorrow. And are, we to believe that poor, helpless man, after being tossed about like a piece of rotten timber on the angry billows of life, is, if he proves too weak to resist them, to be punished by a *sempiternity* of damnation, or even a temporary punishment? Never! Whether a great or an average sinner, good or bad, guilty or innocent, once delivered of the burden of physical life, the tired and worn-out *Manu* ("thinking Ego") has won the right to a period of absolute rest and bliss. The same unerringly wise and just rather than merciful Law, which inflicts upon the incarnated Ego the Karmic punishment for every sin committed during the preceding life on Earth, provided for the now disembodied Entity a long lease of mental rest, i.e., the entire oblivion of every sad event, aye, to the smallest painful thought, that took place in its last life as a personality, leaving in the soul-memory but the reminiscence of that which was bliss, or led to happiness. Plotinus, who said that our body was the true river of Lethe, for "souls plunged into it forget all," meant more than he said. For, as our terrestial body is like Lethe, so is our *celestial body* in Devachan, and much more.

ENQ. Then am I to understand that the murderer, the transgressor of law divine and human in every shape, is allowed to go unpunished?

THEO. Who ever said that? Our philosophy has a doctrine of punishment as stern as that of the most rigid Calvinist, only far more philosophical and consistent with absolute justice. No deed, not even a sinful thought, will go unpunished; the latter more severely even than the former, as a thought is far more potential in creating evil results than even a deed.* We believe in an unerring law of Retribution, called Karma, which asserts itself in a natural concatenation of causes and their unavoidable results.

ENQ. And how, or where, does it act?

THEO. Every labourer is worthy of his hire, saith Wisdom . . . [Thus the] "personality" is no better than a fresh suit of clothes with its specific characteristics, colour, form and qualities; but the *real* man who wears it is the same culprit as of old. It is the *Individuality* who suffers through his "personality." And it is this, and this alone, that can account for the terrible, still only *apparent,* injustice in the distribution of lots in life to man. When your modern philosophers will have succeeded in showing to us a good reason, why so many apparently innocent and good men are born only to suffer during a whole life-time; why so many are born poor unto starvation in the slums of great cities, abandoned by fate and men; why, while these are born in the gutter, others open their eyes to light in palaces; while a noble birth and fortune seem often given to the worst of men and only rarely to the worthy; while there are beggars whose *inner* selves are peers to the highest and noblest of men; when this, and much more, is satisfactorily explained by either your philosophers or theologians, then only, but not till then, you will have the right to reject the theory of reincarnation. The highest and grandest of poets have dimly perceived this truth of truths. Shelley believed in it, Shakespeare must have thought of it when writing on the worthlessness of Brith. Remember his words:

"Why should my birth keep down my mounting spirit?
Are not all creatures subject unto time?
There's legions now of beggars on the earth,
That their original did spring from Kings,
And many monarchs now, whose fathers were
The riff-raff of their age . . . . . ."

Alter the word "fathers" into "Egos" and you will have the truth.[8]

ENQ. But what is Karma?

THEO. As I have said, we consider it as the *Ultimate Law* of the Universe, the source, origin and fount of all other laws which exist

* "Verily, I say unto you, that whosoever looketh at a woman to lust after her, hath committed adultery with her already in his heart." (Matt. 5:28.)

throughout Nature. Karma is the unerring law which adjusts effect to cause, on the physical, mental and spiritual planes of being. As no cause remains without its due effect from greatest to least, from a cosmic disturbance down to the movement of your hand, and as like produces like, *Karma* is that unseen and unknown law *which adjusts wisely, intelligently and equitably* each effect to its cause, tracing the latter back to its producer. Though itself *unknowable,* its action is perceivable.

ENQ. Then it is the "Absolute," the "Unknowable" again, and is not of much value as an explanation of the problems of life?

THEO. On the contrary. For, though we do not know what karma is *per se,* and in its essence, we *do* know *how* it works, and we can define and describe its mode of action with accuracy. We only do *not* know its ultimate *Cause*, just as modern philosophy universally admits that the *ultimate* Cause of anything is "unknowable." . . . the particular conditions of life in which each person finds himself, are nothing more than the retributive Karma which the individual generated in a previous life. We must not lose sight of the fact that every atom is subject to the general law governing the whole body to which it belongs, and here we come upon the wider track of the Karmic law. Do you not perceive that the aggregate of individual Karma becomes that of the nation to which those individuals belong, and further, that the sum total of National Karma is that of the World? . . . it is upon this broad line of Human interdependence that the law of Karma finds its legitimate and equable issue.

ENQ. Do I, then, understand that the law of Karma is not necessarily an individual law?

THEO. That is just what I mean. It is impossible that Karma could readjust the balance of power in the world's life and progress, unless it had a broad and general line of action. It is held as a truth among Theosophists that the interdependence of Humanity is the cause of what is called Distributive Karma, and it is this law which affords the solution to the great question of collective suffering and its relief. It is an occult law, moreover, that no man can rise superior to his feelings, without lifting, be it ever so little, the whole body of which he is an integral part. In the same way, no one can sin, nor suffer the effects of sin, alone. In reality, there is no such thing as "Separateness;" and the nearest approach to that selfish state, which the laws of life permit, is in the intent or motive. . . . When every individual has contributed to the general good what he can of money, of labour, and of ennobling thought, then, and only then, will the balance of National Karma be struck, and until then we have no right nor any reasons for saying that there is more life on the earth than Nature can support. It is reserved for the heroic souls, the Saviours of our Race and Nation, to find out the cause of this unequal pressure of retributive Karma, and by a supreme effort to re-adjust the balance of power, and save the people from a moral ingulfment a thousand times more disastrous and more permanently evil than the like physical catastrophe, in which you seem to see the only possible outlet for this accumulated misery.

ENQ. Well, then, tell me generally how you describe this law of Karma?

THEO. We describe Karma as that Law of re-adjustment which ever tends to restore disturbed equilibrium in the physical, and broken harmony in the moral world. We say that Karma does not act in this or that particular way always; but that it always *does* act so as to restore Harmony and preserve the balance of equilibrium, in virtue of which the Universe exists.

ENQ. Give me an illustration.

THEO. Later on I will give you a full illustration. Think now of a pond. A stone falls into the water and creates disturbing waves. These waves oscillate backwards and forwards till at last, owing to the operation of what physicists call the law of the dissipation of energy, they are brought to rest, and the water returns to its condition of calm tranquillity. Similarly *all* action, on every plane, produces disturbance in the balanced harmony of the Universe, and the vibrations so produced will continue to roll backwards and forwards, if its area is limited, till equilibrium is restored. But since each such disturbance starts from some particular point, it is clear that equilibrium and harmony can only be restored by the reconverging *to the same point* of all the forces which were set in motion from it. And here you have proof that the consequences of a man's deeds, though, etc. must all react upon *himself* with the same force with which they were set in motion.

ENQ. But I see nothing of moral character about this law. It looks to me like the simple physical law that action and re-action are equal and opposite.

THEO. I am not surprised to hear you say that. Europeans have got so much into the ingrained habit of considering right and wrong, good and evil, as matters of an arbitrary code of law laid down either by men, or imposed upon them by a Personal God. We

Theosophists, however, say that "Good" and "Harmony," and "Evil" and "Dis-harmony," are synonymous. Further we maintain that all pain and suffering are results of want of Harmony, and that the one terrible and only cause of the disturbance of Harmony is *selfishness* in some form or another. Hence Karma gives back to every man the *actual consequences* of his own actions, without any regard to their moral character; but since he receives his due for *all*, it is obvious that he will be made to atone for all sufferings which he has caused, just as he will reap in joy and gladness the fruits of all the happiness and harmony he had helped to produce.[9]

THEO . . . . A plant consists of a root, a stem, and many shoots and leaves. As humanity, as a whole, is the stem which grows from the spiritual root, so is the stem the unity of the plant. Hurt the stem and it is obvious that every shoot and leaf will suffer. So it is with mankind.

ENQ. Yes, but if you injure a leaf or a shoot, you do not injure the whole plant.

THEO. And therefore you think that by injuring *one* man you do not injure humanity? But how do *you* know? Are you aware that even materialistic science teaches that any injury, however slight, to a plant will affect the whole course of its future growth and development? Therefore, you are mistaken, and the analogy is perfect. If, however, you overlook the fact that a cut in the finger may often make the whole body suffer, and react on the whole nervous system, I must all the more remind you that there may well be other spiritual laws, operating on plants and animals as well as mankind, although, as you do not recognize their action on plants and animals, you may deny their existence.

ENQ. What laws do you mean?

THEO. We call them Karmic laws; but you will not understand the full meaning of the term unless you study Occultism. However, my argument did not rest on the assumption of these laws, but really on the analogy of the plant. Expand the idea, carry it out to a universal application, and you will soon find that in true philosophy every physical action has its moral and everlasting effect. Hurt a man by doing him bodily harm; you may think that his pain and suffering cannot spread by any means to his neighbours, least of all to men of other nations. We affirm *that it will, in good time*. Therefore, we say, that unless every man is brought to understand and accept *as an axiomatic truth* by wronging one man we wrong not only ourselves but the whole humanity in the long run, no brotherly feelings such as preached by all the great Reformers, pre-eminently by Buddha and Jesus, are possible on earth.[10]

[The following is just a brief statement regarding the science of astrology as it applies to karma]:

. . . We hold that the science of Astrology only determines the *nature of effects,* by a knowledge of the law of magnetic affinities and attractions of the Planetary bodies, but that is the *Karma* of the individual himslf, which places him in that particular magnetic relation.[11]

[The subject of life after death is obviously inextricably bound up with the doctrine of karma. Space allows only these few words]:

THEO. The whole punishment after death, even for the materialist, consists, therefore, in the absence of any reward, and the utter loss of the consciousness of one's bliss and rest. Karma is the child of the terrestrial Ego, the fruit of the actions of the tree which is the objective personality visible to all, as much as the fruit of all the thoughts and even motives of the spiritual "I;" but Karma is also the tender mother, who heals the wounds inflicted by her during the preceding life, before she will begin to torture this Ego by inflicting upon him new ones. If it may be said that there is not a mental or physical suffering in the life of a mortal which is not the direct fruit and consequence of some sin in a preceding existence; on the other hand, since he does not preserve the slightest recollection of it in his actual life, and feels himself not deserving of such punishment, and therefore thinks he suffers for no guilt of his own, this alone is sufficient to entitle the human soul to the fullest consolation, rest, and bliss in his *post-mortem* existence. Death comes to our spiritual selves ever as a deliverer and friend. For the materialist, who, notwithstanding his materialism, was not a bad man, the interval between the two lives will be like the unbroken and placid sleep of a child, either entirely dreamless, or filled with pictures of which he will have no definite perception; while for the average mortal it will be a dream as vivid as life, and full of realistic bliss and visions.

ENQ. Then the personal man must always go on suffering *blindly* the Karmic penalties which the Ego has incurred?

THEO. Not quite so. At the solemn moment of death every man, even when death is sudden, sees the whole of his past life marshalled before him, in its minutest details. For one short instant the *personal* becomes one with the *individual* and all-knowing *Ego*. But this instant is enough to show to him the whole chain of causes which have been at work during his life. He sees and now understands himself as he is, unadorned by flattery or self-decption. He reads his life, remaining as a spectator looking down into the arena he is quitting; he feels and knows the justice of all the suffering that has overtaken him.

ENQ. Does this happen to everyone?

THEO. Without any exception. Very good and holy men see, we are taught, not only the life they are living, but even several preceding lives in which were produced the causes that made them what they were in the life just closing. They recognize the law of Karma in all its majesty and justice.[12]

. . . This Law [of Retribution] — whether Conscious or Unconscious — predestines nothing and no one. It exists from and in Eternity, truly, for it is Eternity itself; and as such, since no act can be co-equal with eternity, it cannot be said to act, for it is Action itself. It is not the Wave which drowns a man, but the personal action of the wretch, who goes deliberately and places himself under the *impersonal* action of the laws that govern the Ocean's motion. Karma creates nothing, nor does it design. It is man who plans creates causes, and Karmic law adjusts the effect; which adjustment is not an act, but universal harmony, tending ever to resume its original position, like a bough, which, bent down too forcibly, rebounds with corresponding vigour. If it happens to dislocate the arm that tried to bend it out of its natural position, shall we say that it is the bough which broke our arm, or that our own folly has brought us to grief? Karma has never sought to destroy intellectual and individual liberty, like the God invented by the Monotheists. It has not involved its decrees in darkness purposely to perplex man; nor shall it punish him who dares to scrutinize its mysteries. On the contrary, he who unveils through study and meditation its intricate paths, and throws light on those dark ways, in the windings of which so many men perish owing to their ignorance of the labyrinth of life, is working for the good of his fellow-men. Karma is an Absolute and Eternal law in the World of manifestation; and there can only be one Absolute, as One eternal ever present Cause, believers in Karma cannot be regarded as Atheists or materialists — still less as fatalists: for Karma is one with the Unknowable, of which it is an aspect in its effects in the phenomenal world.

Intimately, or rather indissolubly, connected with Karma, then, is the law of re-birth, or of the reincarnation of the same spiritual individually in a long, almost interminable, series of personalities.[13]

. . . Ever turn away your gaze from the imperfections of your neighbour and centre rather your attention upon your own short-comings in order to correct them and become wiser. . . . Show not the disparity between claim and action in another man but — whether he be brother or neighbour — rather help him in his arduous walk in life . . . The problem of true theosophy and its great mission is the working out of clear, unequivocal conceptions of ethic ideas and duties which would satisfy most and best the altruistic and right feeling in us; and the modelling of these conceptions for their adaption into such forms of daily life where they may be applied with most equitableness . . . . Such is the common work in view for all who are willing to act on these principles. It is a laborious task and will require strenuous and persevering exertion, but it must lead you insensibly to progress and leave no room for any selfish aspirations outside the limits traced . . . . .[14]

References

[1] H. P. Blavatsky, *The Key to Theosophy,* London and New York: The Theosophical Publishing Society, 1889.

[2] The Theosophical Glossary, London: The Theosophical Publishing Society, 1892.

[3] *The Theosophist,* Adyar, Vol. V, No. 9, June 1884, p. 223; *H. P. Blavatsky Collected Writings,* Ed. by Boris de Zirkoff, Vol. VI, p. 237.

[4] "Mortality and Pantheism," *The Theosophist,* Vol. V, No. 2, Nov. 1883, pp. 33-34; *Collected Writings,* Vol. V, p. 335.

[5] *The Secret Doctrine,* orig. ed., Vol. II, p. 420.

[6] Ibid., Vol. II, p. 3022 fn.

[7] Ibid., Vol. II, p. 303.

[8] Blavatsky, *Key*, pp. 135-142.

[9] Ibid., pp. 201-207.

[10] Ibid., pp. 46-47.

[11] "Faith in Astrology," *The Theosophist,* Vol. VI, No. 5, February 1885, p. 106; *Collected Writings,* Vol. VI, p. 327.

[12] Blavatsky, *Key*, pp. 161-162.

[13] Blavatsky, *The Secret Doctrine,* Vol. II, pp. 304, 306.

[14] "Original Programme" Manuscript, Ostende, Oct. 3rd, 1886; *Collected Writings,* Vol. VI, p. 170.

The Collected Writings, Volumes I through XI, 1874-1889, compiled by Boris de Zirkoff. The Theosophical Publishing House, Adyar, London, Wheaton (Illinois). Other volumes in progress.

The Key to Theosophy. Original edition: The Theosophical Publishing Society, London and New York, 1889; many subsequent editions.

The Secret Doctrine. Original edition in two volumes, The Theosophical Publishing Co., London, New York and Adyar, 1888; many subsequent edition. 6th edition in six volumes, The Theosophical Publishing House, Adyar, 1971.

The Theosophical Glossary. The Theosophical Publishing Society, London, 1892; several subsequent editions.

Lina Psaltis is particularly well known as a student of the writings of H. P. Blavatsky. She has for several years conducted study groups in Theosophy, lectured occasionally, and contributed articles to various theosophical journals. One of her outstanding contributions to theosophical literature is the Quest Book, *Dynamics of the Psychic World,* compiled, with notes, from the writings of H. P. Blavatsky on magic, mediumship, psychism, and the powers of the spirit. Mrs. Psaltis has also been closely associated with Boris de Zirkoff in compiling and editing the H. P. Blavatsky *Collected Writings.*

3.

THE RHYTHMIC RETURN TO EQUILIBRIUM

James S. Perkins

In Ancient Egypt artists created statues and paintings of the Gods with the intent that the Gods should enter and reside in their creations. Hence works of art became sacred objects. Since the Gods were supermundane beings, obedient to cosmic law, any human artists who would represent them had to be cognizant of those imperatives of all true creation, the universal principles, among which are unity, balance, proportion, rhythm, and harmony. These eternals are observed to be actively present in Nature and were known to philosophers and high priests as composing the very foundations of universal order. Special attention was given by the Egyptian artists to balance and symmetrical harmony, which is evident in their constant return to the squared order in their designs, beginning with the design of the pyramids.

To modern students, also, who are interested in the occult aspects of Nature, these principles are of fundamental importance. It is now widely understood that the whole of creation is a progressive unfoldment of Absolute Motion, motion that is cyclic, the impulses of which generate their own return to equilibrium. From the beginning of time, and throughout the evolving movement, this cyclic action and reaction has been ceaseless. The original, primeval impulse, being omnipotent, gave rise to the infinite concatenations of cycles within cycles in ever denser matter, resulting in the multilevel universe as we know it. Within it, all motion is ever seeking to return to balance. At every level, physical, emotional, mental, and spiritual, any cycle's restoration of equilibrium releases its energies into yet greater cycles that are themselves returning to some more inclusive equilibrium, a procedure that leads ultimately to supreme harmony, the end purpose of the universe.

So viewed, the entire cosmic process is simply a movement from an original state of equipoise into creative motion and return to equilibrium. This lawful motion has been noted in various ways in ancient cultures in terms having the equivalent meaning that the word *Karma* has for us today, namely the law of action and reaction. Throughout the ages various interpreters of the law have adapted its meaning to religious creeds and beliefs, particularly in fields of morality and spiritual beneficience, or the reverse. Every enduring religion and philosophy must deal with the distinction between good and evil. The ethical, moral, and spiritual mores, as determined by each religion's ultimate authority, have gained validity insofar as they have embodied or expressed universal principles. In all religions we see in their pronouncements of right and wrong the law of Karma incorporated in one way or another. Further, since the cyclic nature of Karma also invites predictive discernment, this aspect, too, has been employed in prognosticating good and ill fortune. All by-paths stemming from the main highway of true spiritual knowledge beget endless fears, forebodings, and anxieties. The Karma-nemesis of the Greeks, for example, conveyed an ominous foreshadowing of dark furies descending, remindful of certain religious ideas of avenging angels, and the designations of divine wrath upon unrepentant violators of the Law as proclaimed.

An enlightened Occult Science must restore the concept of Karma to its more accurate meaning as an immutable principle in Nature — the principle of balance — that acts eternally and everywhere to return the cycles of action in worlds of matter, as well as of emotions, mind, and spirit, to an equilibrium of universal harmony. Karma neither rewards or punishes. It is a law that brings every action to its right adjustment, a law that can be used beneficially in all of life's situations; but through human ignorance it is a law that more often than not operates to cause suffering, sorrow and destruction.

Divorced from the element of superstition, Karma may be more truly conceived, perhaps, in a modern terminology as the "feed-back" system of the functioning universe; it automatically rectifies inefficient or disharmonious use of the machinery of existence. Man is self-generator of innumerable thought-patterns and desire-impulses, followed by physical acts, each of which becomes a circuit of forces that can be closed only by the reaction that has been generated. We write our own tickets to glory and gloom. Usually our thinking centers mistakenly upon the idea that if we can close the door against threatened adversity, or open some promising window of opportunity, all main problems will disappear. Yet the "karmic mice" materialize out of the very walls to harass us with fresh concerns. No force can break the Divine Order. But as in all arts, so in the art of living, knowledge makes possible a more skillful use of the rectifying law by diligently applying Nature's eternal principles to all mundane existence.

We might view these principles in a natural order of obtainment. If we assume that three is One Source of all life, and given the Absolute Motion of creation, the principle of *unity* is then primary. Universal *order* appears when the Absolute Motion is perceived in its cyclic measurements, numbers, and proportions. *Rhythm* becomes manifest with the repetitive cycles of motion. *Balance* is the unfailing closure of every cycle. *Harmony* proceeds from balance, and is dependent upon it, harmony being what occurs when balance is achieved, namely a momentary alignment with the Source of Life that reveals some new face of Truth. Through harmony every living thing in Nature is flashing its meaning in the total scheme of life. This ceaseless "information service" can be considered therefore among the universal principles, and might naturally be termed *revelation*.

Given the preceding six principles, a seventh appears as the culmination of universal purpose. Innate in all evolving life, is the eternal attraction toward attainment of archetypal perfection. This will-to-perfection is imperative in evolution, having been ceaselessly active throughout the universe from the beginning. It provides the orientation that guides Nature in the slow evolution of all forms and species toward their fulfillment. In man's consciousness, too, this principle is ever operative. The instinct to progress to a better state of affairs, or a more ideal situation, is more than a human hope; it is an urge rooted in the primeval purpose of life. It may be inactive at times but is constantly present and ready, when stimulated, to awaken fresh motivation. We see Man, despite all frustration and denial, ever responding to newborn purpose, a new day, a new age, with new hope eternally springing in his breast — all of which testifies to an obligatory impellent latent in him, as well as in every other living thing, to achieve the perfect state. This universal attraction is viewed here as a seventh principle in Nature — *perfection.*

With these seven principles listed as above, it may be noted that balance is in the central position. Harmony is subsequent to balance. Balance is essential to any manifestation of harmony. There cannot be harmony without balance. This sequence becomes significant when we recall what one of the greatest Adepts in the spiritual sciences has stated, "We recognize but one law in the universe, the law of harmony."[1] Why did he not refer to Karma as the fundamental law? Coming from such a source, the statement alerts one's attention. Why would harmony be singled out as paramount to Karma, or even to unity?

It is true that harmony is the vesture and expression of universal love bringing all forces and forms into true alignment with their cosmic source. Harmony achieved in any creative action renders beautiful with love what is taking place inexorably through the law of balance. Harmony and balance seem to be interwoven, with harmony as the supreme possibility, the crowning attainment that is innate in the action of the law of balance. But harmony awaits the successful employment of balance. A bridge, beautifully designed, may be a harmony and unity of lines and masses on paper, but the actual structure will collapse if the elements that uphold it do not at all times balance the forces bearing upon it. Harmony and unity disappear in the resulting crash. But the principle of balance is instantly reasserted in the bridge's segments lying scattered on the ground, each equilibrized by forces of gravity and inertia. Harmony was not achieved because the principle of balance was not employed successfully. This sequential order of balance and then harmony is again clearly exemplified in any true work of art. A proportionate balance of all the necessary elements has to be properly assembled and arranged prior to the appearance of a harmony of the whole. Harmony, as said, adds to balance the element of love, which makes manifest the reality of unity and beauty. The law of Karma brings all cyclic action back to equilibrium, but how we behave in this action, what we do creatively with love to render it harmonious, is the supreme value in the experience. Harmony is as a divine chariot drawn by the horses of balance and all the other principles. Viewed similarly, perhaps one might think of harmony as the supreme law in the universe.

The enrichment that can come into our lives through a knowledgeable employment of the law of Karma is limitless. Although Karma functions inexorably, as does the law of gravitation, both laws are equally usable for creative and beneficial purposes. It requires hardly more than mere awareness of this law to awaken an appreciable measure of spiritual self-reliance, a virtue that today seems to be disappearing phenomenally, even among advocates of the spiritual life.

With deeper consideration of the universal law that tells us in simplest terms that we will reap what we sow, we are faced with taking into account those larger cycles of reaping that could only have been "sown" in some other time prior to the present lifetime. Clearly, some of our actions that occur under extraordinary circumstances, and which have crucial effect on other people and living things, will have repercussions for good or ill that extend beyond one's present span of life on earth.

A rhythm then, of recurring earth lives would be the most reasonable postulate for equilibrizing these more extensive cycles of adjustment. They would have to evolve through greater time-spans toward ultimate harmony. In fact, it seems that reincarnation is an irrefutable corollary of the cyclic law when applied to the more complex individual situations. Besides, in view of the other principles, a recurrence of earth lives is evidence in the human kingdom of the universal principle of rhythm. Recurrence would also render even more reasonable and evident the principles of harmony, revelation and perfection.

Clear thinking seems to compel us to expand the horizon of life's duration beyond the confining barriers of the birth and death of our present physical body. The more profoundly one realizes the human situation, the more certainly he sees that Reincarnation and Karma are indissolubly linked as though they were the two sides of a single coin. It follows from such a conclusion that man is a being of far greater potentials than he is likely to imagine — a conclusion that calls for recognition of an immortal element in his being. The recognition goes further, in fact, to that of viewing the immortal element as the *Real Self* in man. With this awareness becoming a reality, the path to supreme knowledge lies immediately ahead.

The beginning of wonder in this direction and the accompanying "love of lonely study" are initial stages in a more rapid growth of the soul, and the beginning of man's true enlightenment. For, as Sri Shankaracharya assures us, it is through soul-knowledge alone that the universe shall be known — the universe both visible and invisible. Overriding all is the law of Karma, the principle of balance. From the soul's point of view Karma as a liberating agent because it functions infallibly to return the true fruit of every seed that is sown. Therefore by remote control this law guarantees that man, when he awakens, can be master of his destiny. One may choose a higher path today with very little apparent effect upon the events of his life. However, if he is a true perceiver of the law, there is not only knowledge of, but a growing faith in, its working. Where there is to be any change in life's course the momentum of the previous course has to be overcome. This is where faith in the law must become the factor of safety if the new course is to be pursued. In all of the great structures that man builds in this world, a factor of safety has to be calculated and continually accounted for in the planning. By analogy, if we may think of a successful employment of the law of Karma in structuring a new course of action for ourselves, the factor of safety to be kept active is faith in the law.

Many strange and dramatic instances might be introduced here to support the reality of this law's ceaseless functioning. But a proof that is universally available is at hand. We need only note the basic fears in man: first, the "normal" fear that through some ill fortune life will deprive him of what he has rightfully gained; and second, the fear of time's inevitable reduction through old age, or disaster, of his powers of adulthood and his position in life. The fear of loss of personal accumulations and of reduction to a lesser status of mortal existence testifies to a deeply ingrained uneasiness in us that inevitable justice is wrought for transgressions permitted in the past; and even for forgotten iniquities, inherited from some other time. These are natural fears that stem from the immortal soul's awareness — even though unrecognized by the person — of the action of Karmic law. Instinctively one knows that the progeny bred in all three worlds — mental, emotional, and physical — are attached to us and remain with us, having their growth to fulfillment and final demise via the cyclic law of action and reaction.

Yet this same law used creatively can bring release from such fears of want and loss. To know this positively is the beginning of freedom within the law, which is one of life's greater blessings. Karma works as truly for tapping the inexhaustible resources of the universe, as it does in the delightful balance of energies that unveil a rainbow in the sky. A great poet, who was also a Master of Life, could say with equanimity: "Clouds come floating into my life from other days, no longer to shed rain, or usher storm, but to give colour to my sunset sky."[2] A creative acceptance of life's patterns can grow out of an alert awareness of the eternally constructive purpose in the universe, as so beautifully worded by Sir Edwin Arnold: "Before beginning, and without an end, as space eternal and as surety sure, is fixed a Power Divine which moves to good, only its laws endure."[3]

If the night closes in upon my sunlit days, let me have faith that as surely as I now transform by will and thought the darkness into light within me, dawn will reappear outwardly, and the sunrise follow. It is not to prayers and penitence that I turn in my self-made prisons, but to action, employing the law. Deliverance is to be sought within. Our powers lie there, enticed forth by circumstances arising all about us. Life is the Teacher, yet if the teaching brings only growing strife and lusts, and hurt, succeeded by burdens of sorrow, how may the faded wheel of necessity be reversed? How other than by the creative usage of adversity? My soul is blessed by calamities to my person when these are made to be stepping stones, or wings to spread, aspiring to some happier abode in the Mystery Supreme.

Of all the advantages that a growing understanding of the law of Karma affords, this stirring towards self-transformation is the most rewarding. For it brings personal assurance that the principle of rhythmic return to equilibrium — Karma — will unfold in time the manifestation of universal Harmony.

References

[1] *The Mahatma Letters to A. P. Sinnett,* transcribed and compiled by A. T. Barker, 3rd ed., Adyar: Theosophical Publishing House, 1962, Letter 22.

[2] Rabindranath Tagore.

[3] *The Light of Asia,* Sir Edwin Arnold.

James S. Perkins is a commercial artist by profession, but he has for a number of years given full time to the work of The Theosophical Soceity. He served as National President of The Theosophical Society in America from 1945 to 1960, and as International Vice President from 1962 to 1973. He is the author of numerous published works, his major books being *From Death to Rebirth* and *A Geometry of Space and Consciousness,* both illustrated with his own symbolic drawings and paintings. He and Mrs. Perkins are presently living at The Manor, the theosophical center in Sydney, Australia, of which he is the head.

4.

THE TRANSMUTATION OF KARMA INTO DHARMA

Dane Rudhyar

Everything in the universe enters the field of existence at the place and time to which it 'belongs.' It appears there and then because at that place and time a particular *need* exists which it can meet.

Why can a particular human being fit the need of a particular family, group, or nation — and in general of humanity — at a particular time? Because the sum-total of the series of past experiences, thoughts, and actions which condition what is possible for this human being to accomplish has made of him or her a *potentially* effective answer to the need.

The newborn is conditioned by the past — ancestral, social-historical and/or personal-reincarnational — as the last link in a chain of attempts by the universe (or some may say by God) to successfully meet a particular cosmic need, and thus to perform a specific role on this planet (or any other). This conditioning is the newborn's *karma*. But the task of performing this role in terms of the need of a particular place and time constitutes his or her *dharma*. Thus dharma and karma are the two sides of the coin of individual existence. Karma is constituted by what is *possible* for the newborn by virtue of a long series of past experiences, whether they be successes or failures. Dharma is defined by the precise character and need of the new existential situation in which birth occurred. This dharma requires a human being whose particular karma makes it possible for him or her to perform the dharma.

In terms of karma, the performance of the new dharma is, however, only possible. The performer may be so deeply and irrevocably conditioned by a past series of at least relative failures that these have created an irreversible momentum. The child and growing youth may have been born in so difficult an environment or with such a handicapped body that the effort needed to effectually *decondition* himself or herself and perform the necessary act of total severance from the birth-surroundings is too difficult. All spiritual living, at least for the vanguard of human beings today, is a constant warfare between the pull of an often dim realization of what one is born to perform and the ghosts of a long series of past 'sins' of omission as well as commission. The inertia of the past (karma) makes the mind unable to clearly see the new possibilities for action and thought (dharma) which the birth-situation actually contains. The special character of this dharma made necessary the existence of a particular karmic situation. Karma may have meant a serious illness in youth or polio in midlife, but these *seeming* handicaps to further achievements may have been indispensable for the maturing of the individual charged with the performance of a dharma requiring mental concentration or the exercise of a powerful, independent will.

Karma, I repeat, conditions. It sets limits to possibilities and gives them a particular character; but that character is what is required for the performance of the dharma. Conditioning does not mean predetermination. The fact of being a member of a minority group in a city tenement indicates only what the human being *starts from.* It does not determine whether the person will be a heroin peddler, or through a series of barely recognizable opportunities immediately made use of, a political or business leader. Both possibilities are there. If we look at the situation strictly from the point of view of the human being gradually developing under extremely difficult biological, psychological, and social conditions, we can only see karma at work. Ancient causes have produced new effects which *of themselves* will automatically seek to reproduce similar causes whose power normally will increase at each repetition. But is this the only way to consider any human situation, and in general the sequence of events and activities representing the warp and woof of a universe? Is strict causality the only way of interpreting the immensely complex relatedness of everything to everything?

Causality, as understood by the intellectual and rational mind, refers only to what recently has been called 'horizontal' relationships — relationships between entities operating at essentially the same level. If we believe in a strictly individualistic kind of 'reincarnation' according to which one personality succeeds another, the latter inevitably and automatically inheriting the karma of success and/or failure left by the former at death — and the old Hindu would say condensed in "the last thought before death" — we picture in our mind the relationship between the two persons as a strictly horizontal relation. The Mosaic law, "An eye for an eye," etc., refers to the horizontal relationship between two persons operating at the same phusical level of existence. At this level, an action is followed by a reaction in the opposite direction. This is the principle of mechanical action-reaction, however formulat ed. It is the law of the Newtonian physics.

If we interpret the world strictly and exclusively in terms of horizontal relationships, we are logically compelled to accept the concept of absolute determinism. It has therefore been said that if all the causes operating in the past were known, their effects and the future effects of these acting as causes could also be totally known. The chain of karma would be unbreakable. If it can be broken, transformed, and perhaps altogether dissolved, there must be a transcendent power able not only to observe and understand the nature of the series of causes and effects, but also to affect it — thus to intervene in the process. To intervene means to act from an at least symbolically 'higher' level. Such an action implies a non-karmic relation. This relation is 'vertical,' not horizontal.

In the Christian concept of a divine intervention in human affairs when God sent His Son to redeem a mankind seemingly hopelessly entagled in its not only collective but generic chain of karma (since the original sin).

A vertical relationship between God and mankind-as-a-whole is implied. A similar type of relationship is postulated in the *Bhagavad Gita* when Krishna states that whenever mankind reaches a state of spiritual darkness and ignorance He reappears among men to restore the dharma obscured by the *maya* of horizontal (social and interpersonal) relationship. In Mahayana Buddhism, Gautama, having reached the supremely transcendent state of Nirvana, returns from it to bring some of its light to humanity; and his example is followed by many Boddhisattvas who accept ceaseless rebirths out of sublime compassion for mankind.

This compassion is essentially a vertical relationship. The Hindu ascetic returned from Nirvana should not be considered, strictly speaking, a 'human' being, even if the outer physical appearance remained that of Gautama. As he *relates* himself once more to human beings in a radically transformed way, he acts as an 'agent' of a 'Reality' that not merely transcends our human and physical planetary realm of existence but — and this is the essential point — *encompasses* it wholly.

The concept that the universe is a 'hierarchy of systems' has become increasingly acceptable to the modern scientific mentality. I call the principle of organization operating in such a hierarchy 'holarchy.' From this holarchic point of view, existence operates in terms of wholes — in terms of organized systems of activity and consciousness — which are all lesser wholes within greater wholes and at the same time greater wholes encompassing a myriad of lesser units. At the physical level we see the holarchic series: atoms, molecules, cells, living organisms, planets, solar systems, galaxies, etc. Each new class includes a myriad of entities of the preceding class and is itself one of many components in a still more inclusive class. Such a hierarchy is one of containment — the higher class contains all that belongs to the lower — not (as in the Army or governmental bureaucracy) one of rank in which, while the higher gives orders to the lower, both levels of command are occupied by persons that are equally human.

According to such a holarchic picture, every whole can, and at times must, consciously and deliberately relate itself to both the lesser wholes it contains and the greater whole in which it 'lives, moves and has its being.' Such interrelatedness between a greater whole and the lesser units it contains is evident at the level of national operation. The State passes laws that constantly affect its members, and it also fosters and maintains what we call the national spirit and an official type of culture and way of life. Conversely, each member of the society contributes positively or negatively to the society's welfare and growth or decay.

A holarchic relation of containment thus links a single person to his or her family, social class, nation and culture, and to mankind-as-a-whole. Such a hierarchical series operates fundamentally at the level of what I call *collective psychism*. This collective psychism is, in most instances, deeply rooted in biological or generic factors, but it transcends the strictly physical level and operates in terms of collective feelings and mental-emotional attitudes that are taken for granted and therefore are, to a large extent, compulsive.

When a person emerges from this collective realm and becomes a truly self-reliant, autonomous, and responsible 'individual,' he (or she) most often today finds himself under the control of the structural power that had been needed for such an emergence from the collective psychism: the ego. This is a state of transition, the state symbolized by the Great War between the forces that represent the essentially 'open' and 'closed' ways of life. The way of the ego can be considered closed because the ego generally resists vertical relationship with a greater whole and cares mostly for horizontal relationships it can manipulate to ensure its own security, comfort, and aggrandizement. The open way is, by contrast, pervaded by a willingness to accept vertical relationship with the greater whole of which one is a part. The battle between these two approaches to life is inherently tragic and at times the bitter struggle seems not worth pursuing. But he whose deepest nature resonates to the power of the open way finds himself an Arjuna whose psyche-mind is able to receive and assimilate the truth Krishna presents to him before the battle begins.

Krishna may be seen for an illumined yet frightening instant as the centralized and all-encompassing Will and Form of the universal Whole; but in less exalted moments he is more simply the revealer of dharma. He reveals to Arjuna what this troubled individual *had been born for* — thus his place and function in the greater whole, humanity. It was Arjuna's karma to be born in a situation of constant feudal warfare; but this birth made it possible for him to perform a particular dharma as an important factor in the victory of the open way of consciousness and activity, which was also the way of emergence from a confusing medley of metaphysical systems, the way of spiritual individualization. *Spiritual* individualization: because it was the process of becoming an autonomous, self-reliant, and responsible individual in terms of what India and humanity-as-a-whole *needed* at the time. Krishna revealed what this need was; but Krishna should be understood as simply a metaphor giving a concrete form to the active and transformative relationship of humanity to a particular man, Arjuna.

An Avatar, as an 'agent' of humanity and an answer to its acute need, is a metaphor revealing the possibility of the Greater Whole, humanity, intervening in a situation expressing the temporary triumph of karma over dharma. This intervention has nevertheless to be focused *through* a particular human individual. This individual is a lesser whole within the greater whole of humanity. He or she is the lesser whole that could most effectively *resonate* to the impact of the revelation from the greater whole — the revelation of the need and of how essentially to meet it.

A great leader able to move people acts as an avatar of the nation that gave him or her birth. He (or she) acts in terms of a national need to which he seeks to give a constructive or transformative answer. The action is conditioned by the karma of *both* the nation-as-a-whole and the leader as a person born in specific circumstances. The family and environmental circumstances into which any would-be leader was born and educated represent his or her karma. But his or her dharma is the voice of the nation revealing to him or her the need to which his or her birth provided the necessary requirements making possible an effective answer. It is nevertheless, I repeat, only a potential answer; for the 'called upon' leader may fail. He or she may even refuse to hear the voice or allow the fear it arouses to engender doubts of its authenticity. The mind filled with karmic intertia may initially fasten upon rationalizations to escape the dharma, as did Arjuna's mind. A lesser loyalty may be used by the karma-conditioned consciousness to invalidate the intuitive, yet still dim and uncertain, feeling of what one's 'truth of being' (dharma) is. A poignant feeling of incapacity may arise justifying itself on the basis of the karmic load one has to bear: "Why me, when so many better persons must be available?"

They may not be available. Karmic conditioning is never of itself good or bad for a task. The question is *how to use it.* A well-known and highly creative psychiatrist was once accused by a colleague of being paranoid. He replied, "Of course, I am paranoid. But I have used this paranoia to give power to my determination to make a basic contribution to psychotherapy." Would Franklin D. Roosevelt have been the leader he proved to be, in a time of severe national and world crisis, if he had not accepted the tragedy of his illness as a means to develop willpower and an incradicable sense of destiny?

The key to the spiritual life is indeed the transmutation of karma into dharma. It is the ability to make of the past, as Franklin Roosevelt said, only a prelude to the future — a 'noble' future. Nobility, in the deepest and truest sense of the word, is the capacity to serve the purpose of a Greater Whole-in-the-making; that is, the exteriorization of a new archetypal system of organization whose time to be concretely manifested has come according to the rhythm of social, planetary, or cosmic evolution.

The truly noble person is aware that he or she is performing a part in a historical drama. He or she is a person, yet the noble performance is *transpersonal.* To live a transpersonal life is to live as a person in terms of the inner directives of a Greater Whole of which one intuitively (or perhaps clearly and objectively), knows oneself to be — potentially — and one wills oneself to become fully and effectively a self-dedicated agent. Such a noble life, which is also an essentially heroic life, is the life of dharma. The individual who lives it is the true 'Aryan,' because the Sanskrit temr *Ayra* means 'noble.' It denotes the capacity to make any karmic conditioning serve a creative function; and here to create, simply means to allow the pull toward the future to overcome the inertia of the past.

This past has produced the lesser whole; but the future, if it be true to the fulfillment of the historical need — the need of the moment, at any level of existence — is nothing other than the working out of the process of exteriorization and concretization of a new potentiality of being inherent in the life and function of the greater whole to which the lesser whole is able to effectively relate itself according to the limitations of his or her birth-conditioning.

At any time, the future is, in a sense, present as an archetype — that is, as a potentiality which, sooner or later and in one way or another, will be actualized. It *will be* realized, but (except probably in relatively rare cases) *who* will actualize it, and *how* and *when* it will be perfectly actualized is not 'determined.' It cannot be determined existentially — thus, in terms of exact deeds and particular doers — because the war between the intertia of karma and the creative power of dharma does not have an inevitable result insofar as any one person or collectivity of persons is concerned. There will be failure as well as success; but no failure or success can be 'absolute,' for the very fact of existence includes both — and their conflict. And the failure of one person sooner or later paves the way for the eventual success of another person who is then, as it were, offered the task of taking the place of whoever failed to perform his or her dharma effectively.

The conflict between dharma and karma should be experienced as a dance rather than a war. In a dance the dynamic will and imagination of the dancer constantly struggles against gravitation. The dancer also *uses* gravitation as well as the floor to define the field of the joyous or tragic battle. To collapse on the floor is to accept defeat by gravitation. To play with the antinomy of fall and recovery is to train for the great performance when the dancer will accept direction by the divine choreographer who, in turn, will have imagined a scenario that fills the needs of the Greater Whole, humanity.

Existence is relatedness. But to limit the principle of relationship to its 'horizontal' manifestation is to give to the concept of causality a strictly logical and intellectually binding character. It is to accept Newton's mechanistic view of the universe — the view that triumphed through the 19th century — and to ignore the Einsteinian world of relativity and space-curvature, and Heisenberg's principle of indeterminacy. If we isolate one level of activity and relatedness we can indeed refer every effect to a cause, itself the effect of preceding causes. This leads us inevitably to a God that has to be the First Cause, and as such is incomprehensible because there can be no intelligible 'reason' for an original Act setting the infinite line of cause-and-effect into operation. Thus we are faced with the tragic and self-defeating statement of St. Augustine, *"Credo qiua absurdum"* — I believe because it is absurd.

"Because!" Our minds seem always driven by the compulsion to postulate a cause for the deepest belief that controls the essence of our living. We are driven also by our seemingly inescapable dependence upon the feeling-concept that we are separate and unique individuals who can only relate to other external and equally separate individual entities. Again, this is the Newtonian concept of motion, a motion interpretable in terms of push and pull, of the mechanical action and reaction of separate bits of matter.

We have come at last, in this century, to the realization that nothing is separate from anything else, and that every conceivable entity, micro- or macrocosmic, is related to every other entity at all levels. The basic fact of existence, at any level our minds can imagine, is not only the interrelatedness, but the interpenetration of all there is.

Realizing this, if we still use the term 'karma' we are compelled to identify its ultimate cosmic meaning with that of such an interrelatedness and interpenetration. H. P. Blavatsky stated that the keyword of the 'fourth dimension' — which corresponds to the traditional fourth level or state of consciousness, *turiya* — is indeed 'interpenetration.' At that level, effects act upon causes, just as the future acts upon the past, and Greater Wholes act upon lesser wholes.

Every system of spiritual philosophy accepts the idea that the Divine intervenes in the human. God sends His 'grace' to those who believe in and pray or sacrifice to Him. Boddhisattvas bestow their blessings and spiritual guidance upon the aspiring and 'noble' section of humanity. Holy men give their *baraka* to their disciples. Even the great Medieval mystic, Meister Eckart, said that God needs man as much as man needs God. The future needs the past in order to have something to overcome and a concrete foundation for creativity. The past needs the future in order to become the present; and the present has meaning only in terms of the interplay between past and future.

Anything is possible because all there is is a network of multidimensional relationships. But, at any particular level of existence, the infinite potentiality of being finds itself limited by the mere fact of being defined — i.e., of being given a particular form and rhythm. Karma, as usually understood, is the limitation imposed upon beings existing at the level of our present humanity — the level at which we have to speak of 'choice' between alternatives. But from a cosmic point of view, all 'choices' are being made at all times. They are interrelated and interdependent.

Such a statement does *not* mean that for a particular human being all choices are equally valid. What constitutes the individuality of a human being is the fact that, for him or her, certain choices are constructive — thus future-oriented — while others are inherently destructive or regressive. In a world of constant motion and actualization of new potentialities of being, to refuse to move toward the future is to regress. Evil is essentially the refusal to move toward the future. It is to accept the repetitive inertia of past choices as inevitable or too powerful to oppose. It is to succumb to karma, instead of using what the past had produced as a floor against which to rebound, and of investing this rebounding with a creative, future-engendering meaning.

The Transmutation of Karma Into Dharma

Dane Rudhyar is a Promethean type of philosopher and creative personality who, for over sixty years, has attempted to transform the character of the assumptions and patterns of thinking structuring our way of life and our Western culture. A deep student of Oriental and occult philosophies, he is perhaps most well-known for his extensive, pioneering work, in reformulating astrology along contemporary psychospiritual lines. Yet he is also a composer of vanguard music, only recently receiving its full recognition, a writer of musical and social criticism, poetry, and two published novels. He has most recently turned his attention toward formulating a new, multi-level approach to psychology, in recognition for which two honorary doctorate degrees were conferred upon him in 1980 (his 85th year), by John F. Kennedy University and the California Institute of Transpersonal Psychology. He is the author of more than thirty-fivebooks and over a thousand articles.

5.

KARMA AND REINCARNATION

L. H. Leslie-Smith

The themes of karma and reincarnation have been current and familiar in the East for many centuries. They have been progressively introduced into the West since the founding of The Theosophical Society in 1875 and have now permeated the thought of the world, at any rate as ideas. Whether accepted as hypotheses, beliefs, or possibilities, these subjects can be discussed in any assembly of intelligent persons. The thinking may be vague, for notions will commonly have been gathered from novels, poems, and plays rather than from any considered presentation. But such media have proved excellent for putting forward fresh or unorthodox concepts. Whereas a well prepared and reasoned statement is apt to be rejected out of hand as at variance with conventional thought and belief, the same ideas in the form of entertainment, or in a cultural setting, raise no automatic barriers. The ordinary reactive defenses are bypassed because the challenge is not made in real life but in a kind of fantasy world of the arts.

Obviously, belief has nothing to do with fact. The disbelief of the majority of men cannot make a truth false; and an untrue statement is rendered nonetheless so because the whole world believes it to be correct. Nor can our earnest desire that something may be true affect its validity in the least. Further, it is no use trying to fit facts into some theory. We must seek a postulate that is not only warranted by the facts but is also a reasonable theory that explains things previously obscure. Thus, though half the peoples of the earth believe in reincarnation, that in itself is no reason for accepting the doctrine, but only for carefully examining it, the evidence for it, and its rationale, in order to form our own opinion. This investigation must be done objectively, with a mind free from bias and preconception and an attitude of openness and receptivity, yet with the critical faculty fully alert. Both karma and reincarnation are vast subjects in their complex application, but their general principles are easy to understand. Let us look at them briefly.

That the universe runs according to law has been axiomatic in theosophical thought, and this is now widely accepted in modern thinking. Every discovery of science seems to confirm it so far as the physical world is concerned. Only on such a basis could technologists have achieved the superb feat of putting men on the moon. H. P. Blavatsky said, "Deity is Law and vice-versa." So-called miraculous occurrences are due to the operation or use of some law, within the all-embracing law of nature, of which we are mostly yet ignorant. Enough "miracles" have been performed by physical means in this century to make this clear. Few people, however, have applied this principle to the more subtle psychic realms. Yet when a law is found working at one level of existence, one can be sure that it works correspondingly at all other levels, though seemingly different, perhaps, because operating in other circumstances and conditions. The whole of nature is one, a unity. "As above, so below" is an occult maxim, which is equally true the other way around. Law is fundamental to all existence.

The most important aspect of universal law, according to H. P. Blavatsky, is the law of adjustment, of balance, of causation, called karma. She calls it "the *Ultimate Law* of the Universe, the source, origin and fount of all the laws which exist throughout Nature. Karma is the unerring law which adjusts effect to cause on the physical, mental and spiritual planes of being." Whenever and wherever imbalance is produced, the self-adjusting intelligent "mechanism" comes into play to restore equilibrium. The root meaning of karma is action; hence it applies to the whole of nature, including man, for action is involved in all manifestation.

It is somewhat confusing that the same word is used for the relation of cause to effect in the lower kingdoms of nature as for humanity, where alone "whatsoever a man soweth, that shall he also reap." Karma not only keeps the stars on their courses and every atom in being, but it also adjusts moral relationships resulting from the power of choice, which is one of the distinguishing characteristics of man. H. P. B. gives the difference when she says that karma is the "law of adjustment which ever tends to restore disturbed equilibrium in the physical and broken harmony in the moral world." To A. P. Sinnett, karma was "the law of ethical causation," which would restrict it to the human race; in that context it seems a fair definition. Repeatedly, H. P. B. speaks of the law of retribution. To modern ears this suggests vengeance, but formerly the word included the meaning of compensation or recompense. Having moral significance, this also can apply to human beings.

The doctrine of karma is nowhere more clearly and yet more profoundly expounded than in *The Key to Theosophy,* H. P. Blavatsky, from which the quotations given above and those to follow are taken unless otherwise stated. Universally, "Karma is that unseen and unknown law *which adjusts wisely, intelligently and equitably* each effect to its cause." Humanly, "Karma gives back to every man the actual consequences of his own action." It follows that it is "an unfailing redresser of human injustice; a stern adjuster of wrongs; a retributive law which punishes and rewards with equal impartiality. It is no respecter of persons" and it "can neither be propitiated nor turned aside by prayer." Inexorably thus it achieves not only the Mikado's sublime object of letting "the punishment fit the crime"; it also complements it justly by making the reward fit the merit. We have to take responsibility for our own actions; the law will surely return results to us. The small boy's plea, "He told me to do it," is no excuse; nor is an order from one in authority or that other common plaint, "I didn't mean to do it." Motive is indeed important and must mitigate the moral force of any action, though it cannot affect the physical result.

The general principle is simple. "It does not require metaphysics or education to make a man understand the broad truths of Karma and Reincarnation." It is one of the splendid features of the theosophical philosophy that the general outline can be easily grasped; yet the greatest minds cannot fully comprehend the implications and ramifications. One is apt to think that one knows about karma. But it is not much that one knows.

Since no person can live to himself and is inevitably caught up in human relationships, the application of karma is bound to be complex. For "the aggregate of individual Karma becomes that of the nation to which those individuals belong, and the sum of national Karma is that of the world." And again, "The interdependence of humanity is the cause of what is called Distributive Karma, and it is the law which affords the solution to the great question of collective suffering and its relief." The individual karma of every man and woman is inextricably linked with that of the group, and through the group with the entire human race.

"Karma is the force that impels to Reincarnation, and that Karma is the destiny man weaves for himself." In any one life we sow the seeds of the personality of the next incarnation. That is the hypothesis. Reincarnation is the method by which human karma, at any rate, works. The two are inseparably interwoven.

This concept offers greater understanding of our lives and of those of the people around us. The circumstances that make things easy for some, hard for others, and well-nigh impossible for still others, are karmic — the precise outcome of their own behavior in the past. That, however, is no reason for not giving anyone all the help we can. Indeed, not to do so would be to build an appropriate failure into our future, in this incarnation or another. That is why today is of the utmost importance; not only today, but this hour, this minute, for by what we do this very moment, every present moment, we mold our tomorrow.

The interdependence of mankind involves group and national karma. We are all intimately linked both with the cultural group into which we are born and with the race of nation of which that group is part. Karma of our own making placed us in the setting of a mystique that is the cumulative result of the nation's history — an aura or mental-emotional atmosphere created by untold generations of our forefathers. This brings in distributive karma, by which the doings of a group involve all members of that group, whether or not they approve of them. This could possibly explain the statement that after death the Ego (the reincarnating individuality, not the personality, which modern psychology calls the "ego") receives only "the reward for the unmerited suffering endured during its past incarnation." At any rate, just as none can avoid the results of his own actions, so no one can stay or turn aside the karma of his group. One cannot run away and opt out of it. If its problems are not faced now, one will remain tied to them karmically in future lives, in future nations perhaps, until proper balance is restored. This raises interesting and cogent points. Is the minority that deserts its native land to settle elsewhere a band of heroes or a bunch of escapists? This question becomes more fascinating in the case of those emigrants who in their new world persecuted those who disagreed with them as fiercely as they themselves had been persecuted before they left their homeland.

Karmic forces return to their individual originators; but with the intricate network in any group they would seem likely to meet and be affected by other forces. The result would thus be a modification of the original. Karmic debts have to be paid. Yet, like ordinary ones, may they not sometimes be met by an altruistic benefactor? Can this not also be within the province of distributive karma? H.P.B. says that "no man can rise superior to his individual failings without lifting, be it ever so little, the whole body of which he is an integral part." Thus he eases a little of the "heavy karma of the world," as it has been put, for his fellows and thereby may be said to a small extent to redeem them. Is not this, raised to a superlative degree, what those great men have done who have been called the saviours of mankind?

All students of Theosophy are familiar with a further aspect of universal law: the law of cycles or of periodicity. This is self-evident in nature — ebb and flow, night and day, waking and sleeping, and so on. A period of activity and growth is followed by one of assimilation and rest. Reincarnation is another example of the same process. After death, Devachan. But death is not just the dissolution of the physical body. That is said to be followed by a widely varied period during which base desires are worked out and purged. The successive breaking up of the lower aspects of the personality culminates in the "second death," which marks the end of that mortal personality. All its spiritual aspirations and higher qualities — "eternal qualities such as love and mercy" — are transferred to the Ego. The complex of body, emotions, brain, of each of us, answering to a certain name, will vanish and its various constituents be resolved again into the matter of their respective planes — "dust to dust" at the physical level, and so forth. "Personal consciousness can hardly last longer than the personality itself." Hence a personality can win relative immortality only by rejecting its lower life of personal desire for one of devotion to unselfish service, whose spiritual qualities can be absorbed by the Ego.

Successive personalities are likened to parts in a series of dramas — or comedies — played by the same actor, the reincarnating individuality. This Ego "retains during the Devachanic period merely the essence of the experience of its past earth life or personality"; but "all that constituted during life the *spiritual* bundle of experiences, the noblest aspirations and *unselfish* nature, clings for the time of the Devachanic period of the Ego. The *actor* is so imbued with the role just played that he dreams of it during the whole Devachanic night." So, "collecting from every terrestrial personality, into which Karma forces it to incarnate, the nectar alone of the spiritual qualities and self-consciousness, it unites all these into one whole and emerges from its chrysalis as the glorified *Dhyan Chohan.* So much the worse for the personalities from which it could collec nothing. Such personalities cannot assuredly outlive consciously their terrestrial existence."

The karmic connection between lives is made by *skandhas,* bundles of attributes. These are psychomental link mechanisms by which characteristics are passed from one personality to its successors. They correspond to the DNA, gene, chromosome arrangement of inherited qualities in the physical bodies. They are, as it were, the seeds of character, representing innate faculty and capability — or lack of it. At death they "remain as karmic effects, as germs, in the atmosphere of the terrestrial plane to attach themselves to the new personality of the Ego when it reincarnates."

What of Devachan? "Devachan is a state of mental bliss . . . analogous to but far more vivid and real than the most vivid dream." It is an idealistic and subjective continuation of earth life, a dream world of our own fashioning. The world of this present life is also the creation of our own minds through sense impressions made on the brain — also an illusion, we are told. After the death of Keats, Shelley wrote: "He hath awakened from the dream of life." Are both this life and the post-mortem one simply dreams, seemingly very real, one more highly colored than the other? Again, H. P. B. said "Death is sleep." What relation have sleep and dreams to Reality? These are questions worth pondering. Maybe our concepts need looking at again. We can accept without reservation the validity of the cyclic law, but we may well be cautious with interpretations of its application on the various planes of being and guard against the tendency to fixed ideas.

"The period between births is said to extend to ten to fifteen centuries." *The Mahatma Letters to A. P. Sinnett,* however, gives a hundred times longer "in the transitory sphere of *effects* than on the globes." Was 1,500 reckoned to be a hundred times the average length of life in those days — fifteen years, owing to the high mortality rate in infancy? There is this also: "In eternity the longest periods of time are as the wink of an eye." Then surely a seeming period of fifteen centuries might actually pass in a few minutes, hours, days, weeks. There is no common time scale, and comparisons could easily lead us astray in our thinking. Maybe in meditation sometime a flash of illumination and understanding will come.

The theories, hypotheses, doctrines — as suits us best — of karma and reincarnation present a scheme of law that can throw light on evolution and can make some sense of life and death, rendering the former intelligible and the latter negligible. They show a pattern that explains the world as it is with its many human problems. They offer a unique philosophy for living and an unrivaled basis for moral values.

Human potentialities unfold slowly yet surely under the law of adjustment, which is wholly educative, teaching men by experience until they come to realize their responsibility, not only to their fellows but also to the other kingdoms of nature. Only what is worthy of the immortal centre within each one of us can survive. All the separative qualities — pride, possessiveness, selfishness — have to go. By stripping away these, by discarding the illusory toys on which the world sets great store, a man may return to his native purity of soul, through which divine light and wisdom may be manifested in a human being.

The modern course is for man to take charge of his destiny. Unconsciously he has always been responsible, for present actions mold his future, just as his own past actions have predestined the present. But if we are consciously to shape the future — a task that evolution is steadily forcing on us — then only a knowledge of the great laws of karma and reincarnation can enable us to do so wisely.

L. H. Leslie-Smith, M.C., M.A., is a graduate of Oxford. Now retired, he served for thirty-eight years on the editorial staff of *The Times*, London. He became a member of The Theosophical Society in 1936 and for many years has been on the Executive Committee of the Society of England. He served as General Secretary (President) of the Society in that country from 1965 to 1969. He is Chairman of the Theosophical Publishing House in London and of Tekels Park Estate, Ltd., the theosphical center at Camberley; he is also a member of the International General Council of The Theosophical Society.

6.

THE SOURCE OF BECAUSES

Clarence R. Pedersen

"All things have 'becauses,' " wrote Arthur Koestler in his book, *Act of Creation*,[1] in what may be the most succinct explanation of the *modus operandi* of nature ever offered by a philosopher. For of the many questions which puzzle the mind of man, the concept of karma as cause and effect, or action and reaction, has long been one of the most challenging and disturbing. Throughout history this concept has been debated, described, defied, and denied. It has been the basis of much philosophical theory, religious dogma, and scientific deduction. The ontologist finds this aspect of nature intrinsic to life, for ontology becomes a meaningless science unless karma is incorporated as one of the fundamental aspects of being. Sociologically, karma, even when unrecognized as such has been the rationale behind our concept of justice.

To those who have studied reincarnation as a doctrine essential to the theory of evolution, karma is a most meaningful concept. Regarding karma as action plus the results of action, the student recognizes that the proper consideration of events cannot be complete unless the preceding related activity, plus the sequel to an event, then the sequel to the sequel, *ad infinitum*, are all considered as integral parts of the entire chain of action.

Defining karma in *The Secret Doctrine*,[2] H.P. Blavatsky wrote: "Karma. . . is eternity itself; and as such, since no act can be co-equal with ETERNITY, it cannot be said to act, for it is ACTION itself." It would seem from this definition that karma must have come into operation with the first instant of manifestation, the first instant of creation. For manifestation is action; in addition, it automatically establishes a dichotomy between the source of the creation and the created, a bifurcation which is, so to speak, the very "nature of nature." Thus there is this act of separation which might be termed "First Cause."

According to the theosophical philosophy, it was from this original act of creation that vast numbers of microcosmic units of consciousness, all deriving from the Absolute Principle, began their evolution. Each of these units, being essentially a spark of the Divine, became a microcosmic world in itself, each able to create in its own right by projecting portions of itself into the world outside. It is suggested that as the act of creation by Deity is the beginning of macrocosmic karma, so the first reaching out of the individual soul is the beginning of karma at the microcosmic level. Here too, although on an infinitely smaller scale, there is the creator and the created, with action as the relationship between them. It is implied, of course, that at the earliest stage of evolution, the mental capacities of the units of consciousness are still latent, and thus no personal responsibility is attached to action. In this highly undifferentiated state, karma is simply physical cause and effect, involving groups of dimly conscious units.

Nevertheless, because the superficial diversity of these sparks of consciousness leads to a vast assortment of conflicting creativity, and because the unpolarized noumenon always resists the establishment of polarized phenomena, we find that the projection of consciousness creates an "unnatural" tension, an imbalance within the universe. We note an incessant tug of war throughout creation, first a pulling away from the center of being (centrifugal force), then a compensatory reaction, a pulling back to the center (centripetal force). This rubber band-like quality of nature eliminates imbalance and restores the universal ethic of harmony.

We find further that within the localization of each unit of consciousness, as the personality moves from a state of latency, there is the development of a subjective dichotomy due to the relatedness between various components of the psyche. Here also nature strives to overcome the resulting disharmony.

Thus we find that the act of creation is basically divisive, but that nature, the moment it creates this diversity, immediately demands the reunion of the separate parts.

We may say that there appears to be within nature an exquisite tendency toward maintaining the status quo of pure spirit — spirit unsullied and unencumbered by the matter of manifestation. God, we may say, observing what he has wrought, immediately repents his rashness. Unable to recall that portion of his consciousness which he has willed forth, he now does the next best thing and proceeds to negate the effects of First Cause. It is, then, this need to eliminate polarity which seems to be the "cause" of cause and effect. This is an underlying quality of nature, and its manifested result is the law of compensation.

There have of course been many different interpretations of karma and how it affects life. As with all laws which operate in realms not susceptible to empirical evidence, the various conclusions reached concerning karma have been conditioned by the limited nature of man's knowledge and by his desire to adjust his philosophy to meet his needs and inclinations. Under these limitations, complete objectivity of interpretation is impossible, and so we find that karma frequently means different things to different people.

For instance, many people believe that karmic law is based upon an ethical interpretation of action — that the nature of reaction is dependent upon an evaluation of action in relation to certain ethical standards. As these standards vary with the psychological uniqueness of the individual, they cannot be designated as universal moral imperatives, and it would therefore be inaccurate to interpret karma on this basis.

The belief in karma as an evaluator of the ethics of human behavior has at times led to the conclusion that karmic reaction is instigated by a force or forces extraneous to the perpetrator of the action. Such a conclusion is not surprising if we consider the background of many major religions. Here we find that commandments for ethical behavior have traditionally been "given" to man by Deity. Therefore, karma, accepted in this sense, has also assumed the status of divinity. We find, in the Hindu religion, that the *Lipika* (Lords of Karma) have become the personal karmic administrators in the same way that Jehovah, the God of the Jews, Gentiles, and Moslems, has been personalized as a stern but just God. As an evaluator of ethics, karma has become a guarantee of justice, *as justice is understood from the point of view of the personality;* consequently it has become a concept restricted by the limits of the human psyche.

However, as all action is related either directly or indirectly to First Cause, and as it appears that the nature of the primordial Source reflects an inherent need to expand creativity through the unfoldment of its basic integrative nature, it would appear that action which deviates from this original impulse would be subject to corrective influences. Thus, any action which tends to hurt or dwarf life might be considered unethical, and the reaction might tend to redirect the drive of the actor.

But, if karma is truly the need of the Creator to dispel the polarity of manifestation, this need must perforce apply to *all* activity, and thus it would seem that morality would not be a necessary factor. In this sense, karma would simply be the agent which in effect nullified all action by means of reaction.

One effect of (or reaction to) this ethical interpretation of karma has sometimes been a fear of acting because of the consequences which might follow. Thus we find the development within some people of an inclination toward noninvolvement in the human scene, toward abstinence from action. This manifests in many cases as a strong tendency to live what might be called a "karmaless" existence. This situation might possibly be compared to the germination of a physical antibody, an attempt to instill within the psyche an antikarma serum composed of antiemotional matter, which manifests as a strong desire to repress activity.

Now if we accept the fact that part of the reason for physical incarnation is objective experiencing through relationship, it appears that such a nihilistic approach to life would be contrary to our basic will to act. It seems that life, to fulfill its *dharma* (purpose), must include both subjective and objective activity, the degree of each depending upon the stage of development of the individual Ego.* Thus, inordinate deliberate withdrawal from life would seem to be in opposition to the natural unfoldment of man's consciousness. In other words, man's greatest "sin" might be an attempt to avoid his karma; the attempt by the personality to achieve morality by becoming amoral. Such an attempt to circumvent natural law cannot succeed, of course, for an "attempt" implies action to which there would be a reaction. The karma which would follow this negative approach to life would seem to be in the nature of emotional distortion of the psyche; the result might be that, in the future, before engaging in the normal activity of living, the personality would have to overcome the tendency to repress action. This "need to overcome" would be the karma of the Ego and would presumably manifest in the psyche as a specific attribute based on fear.

"Karma," wrote Arthur Robson in his book, *Look at Your Karma,*[3] "means 'actions,' 'doing,' but is used of those things only that we do by natural impulse, innate tendency. In other words one's karma is the sum of one's habits, tendencies, mannerisms and peculiarities of nature, as manifested in what one does."

According to this definition, it would seem that karma proceeds invariably from the psychic force field of the "doer" and never from the occasion itself; that for the occasion to be reactive, to be an effect of a cause previously traced to the "doer," there must be an active acceptance of the occasion by the "doer," whether this acceptance be positive or negative.

Karma in this sense is simply doing and redoing by the unit of consciousness and makes consciousness synonymous with action. In no way does it imply a reaction by the "not-I." Thus, events emanating from the "not-I" cannot be considered as retributive, edifying, or rewarding in themselves. Rather, their effects upon the psyche depend upon the manner of acceptance by the psyche, and this acceptance is subject to the amplifications or modifications of the will of the center of consciousness.

---

* Understood here as the true identity, the reincarnating entity, rather than the ego as identified in modern psychology.

Examining our concept from this point of view, it might be helpful to divide the consideration of karma into three categories: the karma of anticipation; the karma of realization; the karma of remembrance. This last is, of course, a correlative of the first but is used here in the sense of regretting or enjoying a past activity. There is little room for debating the complete subjectivity of the first and third categories. Anticipation and remembrance of relationships with the "not-I" are qualities unique to each localization of consciousness. This leaves the karma of realization as the only type of karma which might be instigated by outside influences.

However, if we accept the fact that the Ego is autonomous within the limits of its psychic force field, that each unit of consciousness is a self-sustaining microcosm within the limits of macrocosmic law, then it seems logical to conclude that the unfoldment of consciousness is dependent upon the will of the Ego. The Ego is stimulated by outside energies only after it determines the need for a specific relationship and guides the consciousness correspondingly. Frequently such subjective motivation is generated from the deep layers of the unconscious, and thus may not be recognized by the waking consciousness.

Of course, Egoic action implies self-awareness but, as has been suggested, this condition is not manifest at the outset of creation.

Prior to what might be termed the "humanization" of the unit of consciousness, before the mental principle with its quality of reflection and judgment becomes manifest, there appear to be certain general guidelines arranged to direct the consciousness to an environment suitable for its evolutionary needs. Although karma, as action and reaction, is a factor in this "gestation period" of the Ego, there is as yet no self-awareness, and thus no basis for judging action in relation to development needs. Yet there is relative importance in this early activity, for the manner of acceptance by the consciousness of the original outside stimulus is the first transmutation of an attribute, a transmutation from a state of latency to one of manifested activity. The energies used in absorbing this experience will be converted into habit, so that subsequent experience will be correspondingly conditioned. Thus it seems that our first manner of accepting experience might be the most important, much as the training of an infant is more vital than that of later years.

It is suggested however that once consciousness has reached human status, the threads of the web of life are created solely by the Ego. Thereafter, at no time does any outside force penetrate within the "ring pass not" of the evolving consciousness. Indeed such an intrusion would seem to be contrary to the pattern of creation as understood by Theosophy, for inasmuch as the Ego bears complete responsibility for its actions, the will of the Ego, within the limits of natural law, must decide what relationships it should have.

Thus we find that karma is the web of life, the total pattern of cause and effect: causes originated by the Ego; effects depending upon the manner of acceptance by the Ego.

Granting the individual psyche this degree of autonomy helps to change our perspective of the influences of outside forces of human life. No longer will the "Lords of Karma" — a vaguely anthropomorphic group of superhumans — be our personal administrators; rather are we subject only to impersonal principle, to natural law. No longer will parochial morality be confused with the universal ethic. Rather, karma will tend to be accepted as a philosophy of complete self-responsibility, so complete that we ourselves must undertake any necessary corrective measures. We may see more clearly that each of us is a god unto himself; that we must not — nay, cannot — rely on outside circumstance to guide our evolution. For all necessary forces are available to each of us; being essentially divine, we can summon to our assistance the powers of divinity at any time we will. These powers of divinity are essential aspects of our own nature, not a part of life outside ourselves. As Dr. C. G. Jung remarks in his introduction to *The Tibetan Book of the Dead,* "The Soul [or, as here, the individual consciousness] is assuredly not small, but the radiant Godhead itself. . .even the gods are the radiance and reflections of our own souls. . . .The world of gods and spirits is truly 'nothing but' the collective unconscious inside me."[4]

From this it would seem that you as a person are the "doer," the creator of the occasion, or the responder to the occasion, or both. This of course means that there is never an event in the course of evolution which is in any way fortuitous or fatalistic. There is no arbitrariness in action. Purpose predominates. For karma, beginning with creation, will control creation until the time arrives for the Sound of Silence to return once more.

References

[1] Arthur Koestler, *Act of Creation,* New York: The Macmillan Co., 1964, p. 616.

[2] H. P. Blavatsky, *The Secret Doctrine,* Adyar: The Theosophical Publishing House, 1938, vol. 3, p. 306.

[3] Arthur Robson, *Look at Your Karma,* Adyar: Vasanta Press, 1964, p. 2.

[4] W. Y. Evans-Wentz, *The Tibetan Book of the Dead,* New York: Oxford University Press, 1960. Introduction by C. G. Jung, pp. xxxix, li, lii.

Clarence R. Pedersen, Publications and Advertising Manager for the Theosophical Publishing House, Wheaton, has followed a business career, but his avocation has long been the study of philosophy, psychology, and, in particular, Theosophy. He has been a member of The Theosophical Society for a number of years, has served as President of both the Oak Park Branch and the Illinois-Wisconsin Federation of the Society. A thoughtful student of human nature and the problems that confront the world today he is a member of the National Committee on Universal Brotherhood and participated in the formation of "Project Brotherhood Now," a program sponsored by the Society to bring about a greater awareness of the principle of the unity of life.

7.

KARMA AND COSMOS

Laurence J. Bendit

Part One

It is very easy to write or speak glibly about the doctrine of *Karma,* calling it the law of cause and effect, pithily stated in human terms by the Gospel saying that "Whatsoever a man soweth, so shall he also reap"; and so on. The statements are true. But in order to understand their deeper aspects we need to see the matter against a much wider background, that of the Cosmos itself. This Cosmos is a Whole, including everything from the very greatest to the most minute — remembering too that our own conception of great and small is limited by the horizons of our mental capacities, that is, the mind which perceives, at this present stage of the evolutionary pattern. This, in turn, means a mind only partly developed and operating, as a rule, far short of its latent capabilities.

Thus, before we come to karma itself, we should consider a few points relating to the universe we live in. To begin with, we need to see it as a single unit, in whch anything occurring in any part of it influences, in however minute a degree, the rest. A person jumping on the earth, an electron shifting its orbit around an atomic nucleus, a star or galaxy exploding a thousand lightyears away, sends a ripple of some kind throughout the physical universe. And, equally, a mental act of thought, feeling, perception, affects the whole of the psychic or mental and perhaps also the spiritual world.

This Whole, however, operates within its fields as if it were subdivided — "granulated," to use Teilhard's phrase — into an infinite, or at least indefinite number of "monads." A monad can be defined, in line with both Leibnitz, H. P. Blavatsky, and others, as consisting of a nucleus within a field of matter or energies, contained by a "semipermeable membrane" or enclosing skin which at once connects it and separates it from its surroundings. Such a monad may be infinitely small (e.g., an electron) or on as vast a spatial scale as the universe itself. Typically, a single cell such as one of yeast shows us the basic monadic pattern: the nucleus is its creative center, holding the genetic material; the protoplasm is the surrounding field, while the outer membrane allows of a controlled circulation of material between the inner body of the cell and the fluid in which it lives.

In the *Stanzas of Dzyan,* the "skin" is called by the picturesque name of "the Ring Called Pass-Not" or, simply, the "Ring-Pass-Not." It is evident that each monad, great as a cluster of galaxies, small as an electron, is related to a hierarchy of other monads on its own scale or level; greater (as a cell is in an animal or vegetable body); or itself enclosing a number of smaller ones (atoms, molecules, etc.). On this pattern the Creation is built, or so it seems to us.

Before proceeding with our study it will be well if we establish firmly in the back of our minds that any such study can only present us with a relatively real picture of things. Owing to the limitations of our minds, we never see things as they are, but, at best, build up a picture more or less closely related to the actual truth. We do not see the truth itself. The importance of this will become apparent as we go on and it becomes clear that no understanding of our subject can arise until we are capable of combining at least two seemingly divergent forms of mental approach to it. In these the science of causality, which is our traditional Western mode of thinking, becomes wedded to another form of science, where synchronicity — the impact of events on the immediate here and now — is the basis of another kind of philosophy. The latter is mainly derived from Chinese Taoism which, as it were, cuts at right-angles across the linear, time-track habit of the West, adding a new dimension to our way of thinking. This gives a stereoscopic view instead of one that is two-dimensional and flat.

This can best be illustrated when we consider the created and manifested universe which is our present home, even from the level of the physical plane and without going into the less defined and seemingly less organized realm of the psyche or non-physical. For there are two schools of thought among cosmologists today. One sees Creation as an Act (Latin: *Actus* or *Actum*, something done and achieved) in time, hence as having a beginning and an end. Indian thought tells of a "Day of Brahma" or *Manvantara*, lasting so many million years (presumably earth-years). This follows the time-track and is in line with those modern astronomers who see the universe beginning with a "big bang" and gradually running down. But the other school, observing stars exploding, "black holes" appearing in outer space, nebulae condensing into stars — and that within our own lifetime — conceive the universe as in a state of constant becoming: creation, destruction, re-creation which might go on indefinitely. The latter tunes in with the other kind of science, that of Taoism.

One is tempted to take sides, to accept one theory as true, the other as false. But the occultist needs to develop the kind of mind which is able to see that both approaches are true; since time is part of the *maya* or self-created "illusion" by which we live, there is no fundamental contradiction between the synchronistic, Taoist view and that of India and Western science. Together they can serve us in our search; one alone hides Reality and gives us only a blinkered, partial view of things-as-they-are, in truth.

So we can consider that what we call monads are in a constant state of being created, dissolved, and re-created all the time. They can be looked upon as existing off the line of time, as beginningless and endless, or as permanent entities. They exist, moreover, on every time scale, from the momentary one of certain subatomic particles to the apparent everlastingness of a galaxy, or, if not a galaxy, of the physical universe as a whole.

The question is one of our ability to measure time with our mental processes. The same applies to the space-scale as between an electron and a cluster of stars. We do not know in any absolute way what either time or space may be. We know them only as we glimpse them at any NOW and HERE, in the "intersection of the timeless moment."

This, however, is to think only of the physical aspect of a monad, or of those monads which have physical existence. There is also the factor of consciousness, of the fullness or otherwise of the expression of the life within each one. We can, here, speak only in relation to man, the nearest kind of monadic unit to ourselves, and here we believe, rightly or wrongly, that on the evolutionary ladder we are the first to have the potentiality of self-identity, both of being a self-monad, and of knowing ourselves as self-monads. Who can say whether the center of a solar system or even a planet — what we call a god if not God — has anything like what we call a Self and is conscious of it-Self? It would be surprising if Selfhood were limited to such cosmic creatures as earth-men, but we do not know directly, even from the deepest mystical experience centering round our own selves; even if it shows us how much more there is beyond that Self, how much of the Divine remains unknown and unknowable so that it is called the Void and, equally aptly, the Plenum — the opposite of Voidness.

I-ness is the center of man's Being, known in more technical terms as the *Atman* operating through *Manas,* Pure Mind, within the "Ring-Pass-Not" of the physical body during physical incarnation. It is individual at root, yet one has to remember also that it is incorporated in the context of the Cosmos as a whole; it is made up of the same material as this Cosmos, planned on the same archetypal blueprint as every other monad, though the "protoplasmic" elements within its field will be differently arranged and will differ in their power as against one another, because of the individuality which is its nucleus. Morever, these elements may, at any given time, operate in different patterns from their momentary and passing state outside the "Ring-Pass'Not" of an individuality: from what we call Nature, or the world outside us. This differential, however embryonic, in some measure alienates each of us from

Nature and gives us a new relationship to that world. This in turn brings into being a certain stress, a field of force between the individual and "crude, unaided Nature" which, like any other energy field is at least potentially creative of new things.

This, at least in the definition I shall adopt, is where *karma* starts. No self, no karma. Introduce self and that self begins to interact actively with its environment, and that interaction is karma. There are some who speak of animals generating karma but, if this is the case, the term must be further extended to include all forms of action and reaction in any part of the universe. This is logical, but then the idea of karma is equated with the whole field of causality, even if this is entirely mechanical and devoid of any kind of consciousness or self-determination. It seems better to use the word in the narrower sense, as applied to the entity which has at least some degree of identity as a self. At the same time, such an idea has the value of making us realize the total integration of all levels of the world we live in, in terms of universally applicable law. The law of karma is, in the scientific sense, nothing but a "special case" within this universal law.

* * * * *

The idea of man being integral with the world in which he lives brings us to a most important consideration, which takes us back to our ideas on cosmology. Here we can find at least three languages in which we can start thinking thoughts about this universe, each of which embraces the seemingly conflicting pictures presented earlier.

First let us look at the statement made in a kind of shorthand in the *Stanzas of Dzyan*. These — said by H. P. Blavatsky to come from what may be the most ancient document in the world still in existence, hidden away in some remote library — are so obscure that either a highly developed intuition, or such immense commentaries as are contained in Blavatsky's major book are necessary to make them explicit.

We then have science where, at least as regards the physical world, vast progress has been made, especially since the day of Einstein. Surprisingly enough, this has resulted in showing us that matter is not really there at all, that at best something *may* be *somewhere in space at a particular moment of time,* bu that is not so much certain as *probable*. (Incidentally, this discovery has brought some people back to a religious sense of the numinous which no amount of scriptural reading or theology could do. It has also brought into existence a new sacred language, that of Higher Mathematics, intelligible only to its initiates.)

More open to us, because closer to the ordinary mind, is the third approach, that which comes through the study of myth. Here we have a pantheon of beings supposedly immortal and superior to men. These equate with celestial bodies, stars, constellations, and planets, and also with various earth functions or features such as sky, sea, water, earth, and so on. In effect it would seem that when modern science speaks of energy, matter, spin, inertia, mass, gravity, speed, and so on, it really gives new names to the gods. These Gods (in the case of the Greeks especially) not only interfere in human affairs, but are often shown in conflict among themselves. In particular there is the strange idea of the displacement of the "Old Gods" by a new hierarchy, when the Titans, ruled by Kronos, were ousted by Kronos's upstart son, Zeus, and relegated to a remote sphere away from earth and its humanity: a story which can be taken to suggest the stresses and strains inevitable when a solar system breaks out of a galaxy, a planet from a central sun — and, it may be added, when a humanity or human monad becomes differentiated from the mass life of the biosphere and is individualized.

The relevance of this to the doctrine of karma is that man is made up of precisely the same "material" — i.e., forces and energies in one terminology, or of the very same gods in another — as the universe itself. In other words, the pantheon itself is not only outside him but also within. And, like the external world, it is active and dynamic at all levels from the physical "up" or "inward."

In the external world the gods may be said to be organized around a center which we call God. In man they cluster around the nucleus of Self, where they are governed by the same laws as govern the surrounding realms. But the effect of Self may be strong or weak, and so exerts more, or less, influence on the conflicting gods within its field; and conflicting they certainly are, until we learn how to bring them into order, which is the task of what we know, as religion and its disciplines, simple or sophisticated.

Meanwhile, the personality which is made up of these forces interacts with its surroundings and generates karma. Our personal reaction to this is to find some effects pleasant and we call them good, or unpleasant, and we call them bad. In reality, karma is neither good nor bad; it is simply *karma* and is exactly suited to the causes which created it. Indeed, the working of the karmic law may be likened to that of a celestial computer. There is a tradition of certain Agencies known as the *Lipika* or Recording Angels. they do far more than keep ledgers of our acts. They are constantly being programmed with new information which, added to the material stored in their "memory" feeds back on this and alters the resulting impact from moment to moment. This result is in perfect dynamic balance from instant to instant. There is perfect justice throughout the whole universe.

*****

All of this suggests that karma is a somewhat mechanistic process paralleled in Newton's famous law that "to every action there is an equal and opposite reaction." And so it is. Effect follows cause, inevitably. But it is obvious that in many cases a karmic reaction is not immediate, that many "wicked flourish like the green bay tree' and die in full enjoyment of the results of their misdeeds. But karma is not a fixed quantity like the debits or credits entered in an account book. It is made interestingly elastic because of the complexity of factors involved. We have not only the cyclic workings of the mechanical cosmos, we have other and more personal factors less mathematically exact to be placed along the time-track. One can forecast an eclipse or a certain stellar configuration, but one cannot accurately forecast what a living entity such as collective humanity, may do, and so what effects will result, let us say, at the time of some physical or meteorological event.

To a greater or less extent, the individual is involved in wars, revolutions, earthquakes so long as he is human: he seems to have no more free will or ability to choose his fate than the animal kingdom has to act of its own volition in the face of a cataclysmic storm or drought. But this is to forget that man, in addition to his involvement in the collective biosphere, is also a developing individual, within the "Ring-Pass-Not" of his personality. Moreover, unless the intuitions of the multitudes are only wishful thinking and not based on inner knowledge, it would seem that some form of man's individuality is not restricted to time. Following its own cycles, it returns to earth many times before it can become truly free of the "Wheel of Rebirth," after which it determines for itself whether or not it will make use of a new body.

In the meantime, the vast array of cosmic forces is working out its own pattern. In it the individual has his own unique place, and it may be that certain karmic forces do not come into manifest operation until the "slot" in time arrives into which that person fits. It is only as his inner Self takes charge of the personal field that a gradual growth of freedom of choice and will comes into view and modifies the resultant of karmic effects, at any given moment.

We should not think of karma as a fixed quantity so much as a constantly rebalancing and moving pattern impinging on an individual at each moment of time; and, further, that it is one in which individuality plays an increasing part.

This new turn of events is known both to psychologists and to all kinds of religious teachers or *gurus* as a stage in individual self-realization. It starts when the pupil or student comes consciously in touch with what I have called the panteon within, begins to know "how he ticks," and brings the conflicting elements into harmony and order so that they work together instead of as a warring and self-negating mob.

Now, we may say, the processes of karma become reversed. In the past, the individual has been at their mercy, a more or less passive victim of his own acts. Now, however, through what is taking place within him he becomes increasingly able to alter the effects of these past acts on his immediate situation. The gods within become harmonized, and no longer virtually cancel themselves out in conflict but, like a well drilled team, work in increasing unison so that the individual personality brings from within itself a new force which plays into the external pattern of karmic effects. To put it provocatively, the active Self remakes the past from its operational point in the immediate present — something clearly unthinkable if one's mind sees life only from the angel of linear and sequential time. Yet it is not only believed, but known to be so, by the mind which can effectively hold the two views of casuality on the one hand and, on the other, what, for lack of a western word, we call Taoism or synchronistic, co-incidental science (the word co-incidental, being hyphenated, designates the meaningful incidence at a given time and place of the various factors involved in any situation).

The co-incidence of outer and inner events and situations can perhaps best be illustrated by reference to the horoscope of a new-born child. For despite what one scholar described as its "intrinsic improbability," astrology, properly used and understood, has proved to many intelligent people — including Dr. C. G. Jung — that a chart of the heavens at the time of a birth can give endless insight into the child's latent character. And, later in life, because the relation of the stars and planets have changed, it will help to indicate what concatenated "influences" are at work on and in him at any time. This does not mean that the individual is fated from birth to be the slave of his nativity, because, as I have said, the nuclear Self is not a passive onlooker in the development of a character, but plays an increasingly powerful part in the process, as he becomes self-realizing and self-actualizing.

So while it is true that, say, a "badly aspected" Saturn may lead to a frustrated, held-down personality, or Uranus may indicate the likelihood of upheavals and changes, the wise man, by understanding *and accepting* himself in a positive manner, will discover how, by cooperating with the forces in his personality — the gods both within and outside himself — he can change his whole attitude toward life and find harmony and happiness. The Saturn-bound person, when he has performed the magic act of self-acceptance, may find the most obstinate obstacles melt away in a manner which seemed impossible so long as he feared, rejected, or tried to escape from them. The Uranian may find a quiet harmony coming into his life. It is as if the change inside the personality also changes the environment. Or, a physically sick or disabled person may find out how to live happily with his disability, "staying with it" instead of fighting it, and so halving its pain. Victor Frankl, in *Man in Search of Meaning,* points out that the inalienable freedom to *choose one's attitude of mind* persists, even in a Nazi prison camp.

How to bring about this change is an individual matter. But in general terms it comes about as a result of any kind of yoga, including that of psychological analysis of the right kind. The key to it is self-knowledge and self-understanding through deep self-examination.

Happiness is not found by trying to escape suffering but by realizing that it is someting one has evoked by one's own acts. So also is pleasure: one should enjoy ("find joy in") the pleasant things in life, and avoid mortification (to mortify means to kill) from the detached central point which is Self in the deeper sense, not the reflections of that Self in the desire-field of personal ego.

Thus it would seem that the "Man of Tao," or Confucian "Superior Man," the true yogi or rishi, mystic or saint, is one who, in whatever terms, or by whatever method — whether it be meditation or psychological analysis — brings order into the house of his personality. He becomes the arbiter of his own acts. He will still, since he is human, "generate" karma; but not only will he, step by step, learn how to deal with what lies behind him in terms of time; he will find the way to resolve, at the existential instant in which it occurs, any new karma which he creates. Then the back-log, if any, shrinks until it disappears altogether and he is free. He "rules his stars," not by attempting to force his will on the universe, but by learning its laws and becoming its completely obedient servant. In this way, as against that of the prekarmic, premental animal, he will now work from the center of his being as a self-aware, self-understanding individual, the Perfected Man.

* * * * *

To sum up on a practical level, the active, self-actualizing man needs to realize that:

(a) Karma is geared into the whole cosmic process;

(b) It represents the personal and individual impact of this process on himself;

(c) It is his selfhood which initiates the chain of cause and effect which we call karma. This selfhood may be strong or weak, depending on the degree to which he has ordered and taken control of the forces within his personal field. If it is weak, he is carried more or less passively by the ebb and flow of the collective forces around him. If it is strong, he, step-by-step, takes charge of his own destiny.

(d) Selfhood or self-identity is acquired, not by attempts to force matters into the shape one believes one desires, but by understanding and self-awareness. For as one not only knows but, as Teilhard puts it, learns to see oneself in the process of knowing, which has been an indirect, more or less ineffective impact of the true Self on the environment becomes more direct and cooperative with the total cosmic process we know as Nature or God.

(e) To do this well requires a mind developed sufficiently to integrate what, in one aspect, is the duality of the ordinary science of causality with that of what Jung has called synchronicity, or *Tao*.

(f) When this occurs, it is as if, from the immediate *now,* the Self as it were remakes the past, insofar as it changes the immediate impact of ancient causes on the present. The resultant is modified by the Self at the moment when that past impinges on it at any instant of time.

(g) This, clearly, from the immediate instant, influences the future: for the wise man, ideally, deals in a positive way with events as they occur and leaves no backlog of unresolved material to be carried forward. There are no new causal residues to bring out effects at a later date, and the individual becomes free in the deeper sense, ready for the great step which is known as entry into *Nirvana, Moksha,* liberation, or salvation.

(h) Such principles, even if only partially understood and practiced, have an immediate practical lesson for us in our daily lives. For they show us that karma is no accident, but that, in its exactness, we are born at a particular time and a particular place because, whether we like it or not, it is the only proper one, and so the best for us at the time. This should make us think very carefully before we try (as so many do today) to uproot ourselves from our own culture and embrace an alien one, seeking to become Hindus or Zenists or Sufis when we are born in the West; or, in reverse, trying to turn into Europeans or Americans when born in the East. The result is rarely a success, because the would-be convert is in effect a fugutive from the life he has "earned" karmically for himself. He has run away from reality into what, psychologically, is fantasy, however genuine the actual religion or creed he adopts. In general (though there are a few exceptions among individuals who have not fallen into the trap which awaits most of these transvestites), the step they have taken in uprooting themselves from the culture where they belong is backward from, not forward to, Reality. Sooner or later they will have to discover that spiritual freedom is to be found at home, not in a foreign land, however seemingly romantic and "holy" it is supposed to be: to the one who has the eyes to see, London, Los Angeles, and Paris are just as spiritual and holy as Varanasi, Mecca and Jerusalem.

There is another lesson to be learned from karma, which we would do well to introduce into our way of thinking, if not yet into our speech. It is becoming increasingly important today when men and women vie with one another for sexual equality. It is to be hoped that at the back of this there lies a profound intuition, that we are in reality neither men nor women, but human monads, and as such at once sexless and also having the qualities of both masculinity and femininity. But the "Ring-Pass-Not" of the monad is, in each incarnation, sexed as either masculine or feminine; and, since the incarnation represents the fruits of karmic experience, there is a reason why the Self is, for awhile, embodied in a male or female body.

The task of the would-be wise individual is to live with his/her sex, learning the deeper meaning of masculinity or femininity while at the same time not diminishing or reneging on the spiritual and mental qualities of the other sex, but bringing them into play from within. This integrates the masculine or the feminie "unconscious" with the conscious and operative sexuality of the outer garment of that unconsciousness. This is a fact recognized by the better kind of depth psychologist, notably by Jung and his colleagues, where the man's "anima" or the woman's "animus" is taken as an important "archetypal image" in every self-realizing student. A "man" should live like a man while using his feminine intuitions and feelings; a "woman" should be able to be feminine without either weakening her masculinity or trying to become dominant and "masculine" in the wrong way.

This, of course, is a far cry from saying that we should not study other philosophies and religions. On the contrary, the wider our scope the better, provided we add to our mental knowledge the supraintellectual function of understanding, and thus acquire wisdom. What is harmful to the individual is the emotive quality of thinking that, by becoming outwardly a Hidu swami or Buddhist monk or Japanese Zenist, one is liberating oneself from one's karma. At the same time, we need to discover that the Liberation which the serious and realistic seeker is trying to reach can be found anywhere, anytime, when the student is inwardly ready. It is probably so near that we cannot touch it because we reach too far, so obvious that we cannot see it; and, moreover, it may even be that we have already touched it but, with minds full of doctrines, mental concepts, rites and observances, we could over the Vision which our inward eye has given us. Rituals, meditations, disciplines and the like may help, but they do so only for a time. After that they become clogs in the wheel of progress, addictions like that to any other drug. It takes courage to drop all the contents of one's mind, accumulated through aeons of time, and to proceed unfettered into the darkness, relying not even upon a nameless and faceless god, but upon one's own individual Self. Yet, I believe, such is the way in which the individual finds release and mastery over the wheel of rebirth and of karma.

Part Two

There is more to be said about karma than I have written above. For it would seem that the goal of every human being can be summarized by saying that *nirvana, moksha,* liberation, salvation can be reached only when that person is karma-free, that is, when there is no backlog of causes playing into his present state; when he is, so to speak, completely gathered up into the immediate *now.* But so long at least as he is incarnate, his very existence, his presence in the manifested universe, means that he is generating karma at every instant and by his every act, physical or psychic. The difference between such a man and the rest is, however, that he has found the means to resolve this karma at the very instant it is generated and he passes from moment to moment in time.

In principle, this means that he has learned to attune himself absolutely to the cosmic pattern as it is at that moment so that there is no kind of stress or conflict between what is taking place within his individual monadic field and what is happening in the universe as a whole.

Whatever we look upon the universe as proceeding through time from past to future, or whether we see it as a constant dynamic state in which creation and destruction (or better, resolution) are always at work together, each fleeting moment can be seen as an integrated whole of which we are a part. Our job, then, is to bring ourselves into step with the universal rhythm and to keep pace with its forward movement. This is the whole purpose behind what we know as religion and *should* be the aim of all religious creeds and disciplines.

In other words, there is a personal and individual impact of karma, in the greater sense of movement in the cosmos, on our own individual monadic field. This field, as I have suggested, centers round its own "sun" or "god," the true Self, and it is because this Self is not yet in command of its field that man finds himself in trouble, out of tune with the world in which he lives. He will suffer for this until harmony is restored, not because God punishes, but because free will enables him to act differently from other monads, both on his own level and at the levels which contain him (e.g., the biosphere of the earth, the solar system and so on). Erich Fromm has said that the first genuinely human act was when, in Eden, Adam and Eve disobeyed Nature (God) and asserted themselves in such a way that they cut across the laws of prehumanity, thus beginning the long karmic road.

Man's task is thus to restore himself to a state of nature, of harmony with the world, to return to God — without, however, losing the precious things he has acquired during his "estrangement." One of these is individuality, the sense of Selfhood, which distinguishes him from the prehuman animal.

This Selfhood, however, has to become something very different from the little selfhood of the psychological ego, which is constantly obtruding itself and interfering with events in daily life, demanding the fulfilment of instinctive desire.

The process of extracting Self from egoism is the aim of every true religious school. Moreover, as the student moves along the paths laid down by these religions, he has step by step to find his own individual discipline and proceed alone and unaided except from within himself.

It is here that the modern schools of the deepest of depth psychology can be of immense use, because (thanks to Freud, however much we may disagree with his interpretations) they teach us to confront ourselves, and suggest the means of "getting at" the unknown side of ourselves which we call the unconscious. The same could, in theory, be done by a direct study of the forces, psychic and physical, named by science but known more intimately to us as archetypal images of gods, heroes, symbols. A valuable way to begin on this way is that adumbrated by Freud in his *Psychopathology of Everyday Life* — even if we find his preoccupation with the physical body inadequate and tiresome. For he draws our attention to the meaningfulness of mistakes, slips of the tongue, and the "irrational" world of dreams and fantasies. We find meaning in these things when we learn to study them; and they will start us on the discovery of this inner field around the Self, the unconscious. One needs to go through this state; it leads on to what are really the grass roots of man's actual quality.

Now we begin to meet with the essential Man, in the form of what Jung has called the archetypal images: the gods of the pantheon within us, figures of power and charismatic value which are capable, as we allow them to operate on and in us, of carrying us from the realm of *the gods* to that of *God*, the numinous Source of all things. We are, in other words, entering the world of myth, that is, of the deeper truths about ourselves and our origins as human entities. Myth has been said by Annie Besant, as well as by C. G. Jung, to be the true history of man both individual and as a species, and to represent his attempts at spiritual self-realization in the form of dramatic stories.

As we learn about myth as applied to each of us individually, we begin to take control over our destinies, i.e., of our relationship to the Cosmic Myth which is the Universe as a whole. This is worth realizing, as it is clearly much closer to our daily experience to think in terms of myth and of gods and goddesses, of symbols and sacramental acts and objects, than to use the languages of physics and mathematics. For while they are equally valid, they are much more remote for the ordinary individual.

Each of us, as a monad, is the expression of a personal and individual myth; it is for each of us to fulfill and complete that myth in terms of the personal, subjective drama we touch in our dreams, visions, inner experiences. For as we work it out, we bring our nuclear Self into its true place as the center of our personal lives. Also, by ordering the "gods" within us, we catch up, as it were, with the cosmic situation as it moves from moment to moment in constant flow, and so find at once complete freedom, the "liberation" so often spoken of today. But, paradoxically, we do so by becoming completely obedient and at one with the world we call external to our personal monadic selves. This, in another way, is to say that we free ourselves from the law of karma by becoming part of the universal karma which is the very life of a manifested Godhead.

What it amounts to is that we cannot know God without knowing and understanding the gods: those gods which are both cosmic forces and forces within our own monadic sphere. We may know all the teachings about the universe (I use the word "teachings" rather than "fact" because most of the facts about the cosmos are quite beyond our immediate experience, and so have to be taken as unproved hypotheses) but they will have little value or significance to us unless we know our own home-self, our own domestic gods, the actors in the individual myth which is each one of us. The fact that (like the monadic principle outlined earlier in this article) this myth is based on the same blueprint (*see* comparative mythology and its exegesis in psychological and religious texts) with the same basic figures of hero, villain, demonic forces, redeemer, etc., does not detract from this principle. The pantheon is in us, but it functions in its own individual way, this way being linked with the general pattern exhibited in the universe at any moment of time.

As these gods represent karma in a cosmic sense, so do they represent karma in relation to our own individuality. Liberation and ***nirvana*** ("the cessation of error and of strife") comes when the individual monadic pattern harmonizes with the cosmic one and so becomes integrated with it. We are then "united with God the Father" and so become the pattern of the universal Chirst or Buddha.

Suggested Reading

The Stanzas of Dzyan
The major works of H. P. Blavatsky.
The major writings of J. Krishnamurti.
The major works of C. G. Jung.
Experiment in Depth by P. W. Martin (Routledge, London).
Cutting Through Spiritual Materialism by Chogyam Trungpa (Shamballa).
Patterns of Prophecy, Alan Vaughan (Turnstone, London).
Essays by Albert Einstein, Fred Hoyle, and other modern scientists.
The Symbolic and the Real by Ira Progoff.
The Psychopathology of Everday Life; The Interpretation of Dreams by Sigmund Freud (various publishers).

Laurence J. Bendit, psychiatrist, lecturer, and author, held the degrees of M.A., M.D., and B. Chir (i.e. Surgery) from Cambridge University, as well as other British medical diplomas including that of specialist in psychological medicine. Before his death in September of 1974, he made a substantial contribution to the literature of psychology and Theosophy. Among his best known works are *Self-Knowledge, a Yoga for the West, The Mirror of Life and Death* and, with his late wife, Phoebe D. Bendit, *The Psychic Sense* and *This World and That.* His writings appeared frequently in theosophical journals through the world.

8.

INFINITE CONTINUITY IN MULTIMILLIONFOLD DIVERSITY

Arthur Robson

Infinite continuity, but *not* on a level, nor in a dead straight line. We find everywhere this constantly recurring theme of the periodicity of nature, activity alternating with inactivity; broad daylight with its round of activity, followed by night and sleep or comparative inactivity; spring and summer with their growth and activity followed by autumn and winter and cold and a slackening off; birth, youth, and the activities of vigorous manhood or womanhood, and then old age and finally death. There are still larger circles which we discern: the gradual rise of a nation, for example, with a flowering of the arts, literature, commerce etc., followed by its gradual decline and fall. Then we observe that an age of enlightenment, enduring for about a millennium, is followed by a dark age enduring for approximately another millennium. And there are larger circles still, which tell us of warm periods in the life of our planet, alternating with ice ages, when its life was reduced to a minimum.

Why then should we be surprised when we are told that life is a continual ebb and flow, which goes on from one incarnation to another, from life in one body, through death and a period in Devachan ("which may last for years, decades, centuries and millenniums, of ten-times multiplied by something more. It all depends upon the duration of Karma.")[1] to life in another body.

Now, do not make the mistake of confusing this with the idea of transmigration of souls, according to which when one dies one may be born again as a bird or beast. In Shakespeare's *Merchant of Venice* Gratiano says:

> Thou almost mak'st me waver in my faith,
> To hold opinion with Pythagoras,
> That souls of animals infuse themselves
> Into the trunks of men.

Some people see this to be a declaration of the theory of transmigration of souls. But such a theory is against the normal order of things, and Pythagoras never held it. He held, it is true, that "the souls of animals infuse themselves into the trunks of men," but *not the other way about,* which is what the transmigration of souls implies. Once we have attained to life as a human being, we never revert to incarnation as animals.

The common objection to the theory of reincarnation is, "Why don't we remember our past lives?" It's true that ordinarily we cannot recall any part of our past lives, but in everything we do our past is plainly seen. Obvious examples are the natural inclinations of each of us, each characteristically different in its own way, outstanding among them being great musicians, artists, mathematicians, etc., too numerous to catalogue. Some may say, "If I had had the opportunity and devoted myself to it, I could have become as great as X." But is this true? No. The greatness of X has grown by his repeatedly doing through countless lives the things in which he excels. We have to get rid of the notion that such an excellence is a "talent" or "gift." Such "gifts" come from one's having sown well and truly through many lives and, in due course of time, reaping the fruit of that sowing.

There is not a single trait of character, not a mannerism, but has its history — often a history full of events and absorbing interest — the beginnings of which lie so far back in time that the thought of trying to discover them is staggering. It is this mass of habits, mannerisms, and peculiarities of our natures, that which we know as "character," that constitutes our Karma, the record of our entire past, the fount and origin of all the pleasure and pain that we experience. So we get a multimillionfold diversity, as each person has a character which is individually *his own*. And so it will remain till the end of time, because no one can change his nature, although we go on *evolving from within*. The *Bhagavad Gita* tells us:

> Therefore, without attachment, do Karma that is necessary, for by doing Karma without attachment man obtains supreme bliss. As the ignorant act from attachment to Karma, O Bharata, so should the wise act without attachment, having the common welfare at heart.[2]

The Mahatma K. H. has written:

> Your acts in the past . . . cannot be obliterated, for they are indelibly stamped upon the record of Karma.[3]

It is this that we take with us from one life to another. Each trait of character is but a little eddy that goes down the years with us, circling in our life long after the original circumstances that called it into being have been left behind and completely forgotten. Dr. Ananda Coomaraswamy, in speaking of "the momentum of antecedent karma," refers to "the brilliant simile of the potter's wheel, which continues to turn after the hand of the potter is removed."

The word "Karma" comes from the Sanskrit term for "doing," and it is used of all that we do habitually. Of course, we must not only take into consideration the Karma of *merit*, but also that of *demerit*, earned by our past misdeeds.

As the doctrines of Reincarnation and Karma have been revived during the last hundred years, largely through the efforts of The Theosophical Society, it would be well to see how that Society came to be founded.

> After nearly a century of fruitless search, our chiefs had to avail themselves of the only opportunity to send out a European *body* upon European soil to serve as a connecting link between that country and our own.[4]

Thus it was that Russian-born H. P. Blavatsky, after being instructed by the Mahatmas in a secluded valley in the Himalayas, joined with Henry Steel Olcott in the United States of America in founding The Theosophical Society in New York in 1875. This was a unique opportunity to spread the wisdom of the Sages throughout the world.

H. P. Blavatsky wrote *Isis Unveiled* in 1877, and followed it with *The Secret Doctrine* in 1888; each work contained a wealth of most diversified information. Meanwhile the Mahatmas M. and K. H., who had contact with two English gentlemen, A. P. Sinnett and A. O. Hume, and had entered into correspondence with them, were disseminating the same truths through them. Although it was not intended that the letters should be published without having been first edited by a competent authority, they have come to us unedited as *The Mahatma Letters to A. P. Sinnett,* published in 1923, about forty years after they were written.

Let me say straight away that the Mahatmas have no place for the usual ideal of God in their philosophy.

> The word "God" was invented to designate the unknown cause of those effects which man has either admired or dreaded without understanding them, and since we claim that we are able to prove what we claim — i.e., the knowledge of that cause and causes — we are in a position to maintain there is no God or Gods behind them.[5]

But this does not mean that there is no room for supernormal beings in occult philosophy.

> We believe in Dhyan Chohans or Planetaries, and endow them with a universal mind.[6]

But they all form part of the One Life and there is nothing outside it, which an extraterrestrial God would have to be. Even the highest Planetaries were, at some time in the remote past, mortal men such as we; and although they are now supernormal, they passed millions of millions of years ago through the same round of evolutionary growth as we are undergoing today.

Dhyan Chohan (pronounced "Jan Chohan," the "J" being given the same phonetic value as in English words) means "Lord of Wisdom," and corresponds vaguely to the Angels of Christian belief. Planetaries are higher still, and may be said to correspond to Archangels.

It is so very difficult to give an idea of what we are trying to describe except by quoting the master K.H. who says:

> We will perhaps be near correct to call it *infinite life* and the source of all life, visible and invisible, an essence inexhaustible, ever present, in short Swabhavat. (Swabhavat in its universal application, Fohat when manifesting throughout our phenomenal world, or rather the visible universe, hence in its limitations.)[7]

"Swabhavat" is Sanskrit for "self-existent." "Fohat" is a Turanian word which seems to have been derived from "Swabhavat," the initial, unstressed syllable (*swa*) having been elided, and the rest (*bhavat*) having been corrupted to suit linguistic demands, and limited in its application to our visible universe. So Swabhavat is the *infinite life* of which we form part. H. P. Blavatsky says:

> Throughout the first two parts it has been shown that, at the first flutter of renascent life Swabhavat passes, at every new rebirth of Kosmos, from an inactive state into one of intense activity; that it differentiates, and then begins its work through differentiation. This work is KARMA.[8]

This means that Swabhavat goes through much the same process as before the old Kosmos passed out of existence; it is, remember, the same infinite life, and the birth of a new Kosmos is much the same as the birth of a new day, or the birth of a new life, when one returns to one's usual activities. The only God in all this is the "God within my breast." This truth is so stupendous that we find it hard to take it in. Yet there was one who, with Olympian wisdom, perceived it for herself and, furthermore, in Orphean tones proclaimed it for all to hear, even at the risk of being considered shockingly presumptuous and sacrilegious.

IMMORTALITY

No coward soul is mine,
No trembler on the world's storm-troubled sphere;
I see Heaven's glories shine
And faith shines equal, arming me from fear.
O God within my breast,
Almightly, ever-present Deity!
Life — that in me has rest,
As I — undying Life — have power in thee!
Vain are the thousand creeds
That move men's heart; unutterably vain:
Worthless as withered weeds,
Or idlest froth amid the boundless main,
To waken doubt in one
Holding so fast by Thy infinity;
So surely anchored on
The steadfast rock of immortality.
With wide-embracing love
Thy spirit animates eternal years,
Pervades and broods above,
Changes, sustains, dissolves, creates and rears.
Though earth and man were gone,
And suns and universes ceased to be,
And Thou wert left alone,
Every Existence would exist in Thee.
There is not room for Death,
Nor atom that his might could render void;
Thou — THOU are Being and breath,
And what THOU art may never be destroyed.

Emily Bronte.*

* This splendid poem has been set to music in *Six Songs to Poems of Emily Bronte* by John Joubert, obtainable from Novello & Co., Borough Green, Sevenoaks, Kent TW 15 8DT, England.

Set your heart at rest. The sky is the limit, if I may borrow a cliché from television. You may go on evolving until eternity. In fact you *have* to go on evolving, and chiefly *by your own efforts.* The Mahatma M. has written:

> The task is difficult and K.H., in remembrance of old times, when he loved to quote poetry, asks me to close my letter with the following to your address:
>
> Does the road wind up-hill all the way?
> Yes, to the very end.
> Will the day's journey take the whole long day?
> From morn to night, my friend.
>
> Knowledge for the mind, like food for the body, is intended to feed and help growth, but it requires to be well digested, and the more thoroughly and slowly the process is carried out, the better both for the body and the mind.[9]

There is no easy road to Adeptship. The Mahatma K.H. has written:

> The fact is that to the last and supreme initiation every chela (and even some adepts) is left to his own device and counsel. We have to fight our own battles, and the familiar adage — "the adept *becomes,* he is not *made*" — is true to the letter. Since every one of us is the *creator* and producer of the cause that leads to such or some other results, we have to reap but what we have sown.[10]

According to this, it may seem that Adepts are rather callous, leaving chelas (and also some Adepts, who insist on working things out for themselves) to their own devices. On the contrary, they are filled with a most intense compassion, and do what is best for us. What would you do if you noticed an unhatched chicken trying to peck its way out of its egg? To remove the eggshell would result in premature exposure and the chicken would be so much the weaker. No, let it peck its own way out of the shell, as the mother hen lets it do, while she clucks encouragement. The same applies to a man trying to break his way into Adeptship. The sincere aspirant would very much prefer to be left to work his way unassisted.

To understand this let us follow the course of evolution. Until the animal stage one has been entirely under the influence of

Brahma. Nor Brahma is not a god, nor is it a person, nor any other being. Brahma is only an idea, the expansive force of nature. The Mahatma M. has defined the word:

> Brahma, from the root "brih," the Sanskrit for "to expand, grow or fructify," Brahma being but the vivifying *expansive* force of nature in its eternal evolution.[11]

In all animals we find the natural impulse to expand. In the human being this remains for a long time the dominant urge. We find him increasing his wealth, his influence, his power, his knowledge, his skill. But at the same time he learns to be of increasing service to others in many ways. After all, social life becomes ever more interdependent. A new force has become apparent, that of Vishnu, from the Sanskrit *vish,* meaning "to serve." Vishnu is not a god, any more than is Brahma. At first it is inseparable from Brahma. People do service only because *it pays them.* Coal owners and miners, electric boards and electricians, railway boards and railwaymen, etc., all insist on getting as much as they can out of their activities. The countries that produce oil, sugar, etc., hold out for the highest prices obtainable. There is little "service" about it, and the scramble for more and more of what each can get leads to further and further inflation, sending up the prices higher and higher. There is only one way to stop all this, and that is by people of real good will with a true sense of service declining to take more than they really need.

Well, suppose that we were truly *social* and the spirit of service came into its own! Then we should have a true reign of Vishnu, everybody doing all they could to assist wherever they could — the teacher, merchant, manufacturer, judge, etc., all giving of their best. Would everybody be forever happy? Apparently not. Certainly not for very long. Many would prefer to do things for themselves. Now a new force would be required in the Guru, that of detachment, Shiva, a force which allows him to stand aside and allow others to work things out for themselves. We all tend, after having reached a particular stage in our evolution, to identify ourselves with Shiva. The Adept lives in this state almost continuously.

> The adept sees and feels and lives in the very source of all fundamental truths — the Universal Spiritual Essence of Nature, Shiva, the Creator, the Destroyer and the Regenerator. As Spiritualists of today have degraded "Spirit," so have the Hindus degraded Nature by the anthropomorphistic conceptions of it.[12]

The editors of the third edition of the *Letters* have altered the word, "anthropomorphistic" to "anthropomorphic." But in so doing they have missed the whole point of the Mahatma's having to coin a word to convey his meaning. A figure with four faces or four arms is certainly *not* in human form, and can only be said to be in "humanized" form.

Shiva is said to be the Destroyer, but the *Destroyer of Karma.* Shiva is the embodiment of *sacrifice,* and in sacrifice one approaches the divine.

It may be thought that when an Adept attains Nirvana he turns his back on life as something with which he has finished and which no longer concerns him. But, paradoxical as it may seem, he is enabled to withdraw completely from life only because of his having completely merged himself in, and attained perfect At-one-ment, with life The Mahatma K. H. has written:

> Oh, for the final Rest! For that Nirvana where — "to be one with Life, yet — to live not."[13] [But this] State of absolute Rest in which all things objective are forgotten[14]

does not last forever. In due course the Nirvanee returns to consciousness of objective life as a Dhyan Chohan.

Although the Dhyan Chohans have attained complete detachment from life, they do not remain spectators of it. The Mahatma speaks of them as "the protectors of our Race and the Trustees for those that are coming."[15]

Elsewhere the Mahatma, speaking of the animal and vegetable kingdoms, says:

As we have our Dhyan Chohans so have they in their several kingdoms elemental guardians and are well taken care of in the mass as is humanity in the mass.[16]

The Dhyan Chohans take care, not only of the living humanity, but also of the disembodied egos.

Every such "world" within the Sphere of Effects has a Tathagata, or "Dhyan Chohan" to protect and watch over, not to interfere with it.[17]

They protect the victims of accident and murder.

The Dhyan Chohans who have no hand in the guidance of the *living* human Ego, protect the helpless victim when it is violently thrust out of its element into a new one, before it is matured and made fit and ready for it.[18]

They guide the birth-seeking ego to the place of its rebirth:

And it is that variety which guides the temporary personal *Ego* into the current which will lead him to be reborn in a lower or higher condition in the next world of causes. Everything is so harmoniously adjusted in nature — especially in the subjective world — that no mistake can ever be committed by the Tathagatas — or Dhyan Chohans — who guide the impulses.[19]

They not only watch life which is already in being, but also give the impulse which goes to the making of new systems of life.

At the beginning of the solar manwantara the hitherto subjective elements of the material world now scattered in cosmic dust — receiving their impulse from the new Dhyan Chohans of the solar system (the highest of the old ones having gone higher) — will form into primordial ripples of life, and separating into differentiating centres of activity combine in a graduated scale of seven stages of evolution.[20]

They do not *create* a new solar system, any more than a gardener creates a plant when he sows a seed, and so initiates the life cycle of a plant. The cosmic atom is *in itself* potentially a

Dhyan Chohan, just as much as the seed is potentially a plant and, just as the gardener creates conditions which are favorable to the potentiality in the seed developing into reality, so do the Dhyan Chohans create conditions which allow of the cosmic atoms starting on the long road of evolution which leads up to the Dhyan Chohan, or Planetary Spirit.

> The potentiality which develops finally in a perfected planetary spirit lurks in, *is* in fact that primordial cosmic atom.[21]

It is this potentiality that gradually unfolds itself *from within* — "evolutes" — and, having attained humanhood, goes on evoluting until it appears as a perfect Planetary Spirit.

> Evoluting from cosmic matter — which is *akasa,* the primeval not the secondary plastic medium, or Ether of Science instinctively suspected, unproven as the rest — màn first evolutes from this *matter* in its most sublimated state, appearing at the threshold of Eternity as a perfectly *Etherial* — not Spiritual Entity, say — a Planetary Spirit.[22]

A Dhyan Chohan seems to us an absolutely perfect being. But there are degrees of perfection even among them. This is very hard for us to conceive, but the following would probably be an analogy.

We may describe any person as a tightrope walker when he has attained sufficient skill to be able to walk the rope without falling off. This corresponds to Nirvana. But there are refinements in the tightrope walker's art which he will go on acquiring. Similarly, a Dhyan Chohan, having attained Nirvana, acquires immunity from falling back into the round of birth and death. But there are refinements of spirituality which he goes on acquiring after that. Having already learnt to dispense with a physical body, he learns to dispense with one after another of the superphysical bodies, and so becomes in time formless, an "*Arupa*-deva" or formless Dhyan Chohan, the whole process taking a manvantara. What becomes of the Dhyan Chohan, after they become formless is a mystery even to the Adepts.

> As to the winner of that race throughout the worlds — the Spiritual Ego, he will ascend from star to star, from one world to another, circling onward to rebecome the once pure Planetary

> Spirit, then higher still, to finally reach its first starting point, then — to merge into MYSTERY. No adept has ever penetrated beyond the veil of primitive Kosmic matter. The highest, the most perfect vision is limited to the universe of *Form* and *Matter*.[23]

References

1. *The Mahatma Letters to A. P. Sinnett*, transcribed and compiled by A. T. Barker, 3rd ed., Adyar: Theosophical Publishing House, 1962, p. 103.
2. *The Bhagavad Gita*, III: 19, 25.
3. Letters from the Masters of the Wisdom, 2nd Series, p. 61.
4. Barker, op.cit., p. 201.
5. Ibid., p. 52.
6. Ibid., p. 55.
7. Ibid., p. 89.
8. *The Secret Doctrine*, 3rd ed., I:695.
9. Barker, op.cit., p. 258.
10. Ibid., p. 305.
11. Ibid., p. 71.
12. Ibid., p. 241.
13. Ibid., p. 113.
14. Ibid., p. 195.
15. Ibid., p. 154.
16. Ibid., p. 95.
17. Ibid., p. 105.
18. Ibid., p. 128.
19. Ibid., p. 100.
20. Ibid., p. 96.
21. Ibid., p. 88.
22. Ibid., p. 45.
23. Ibid., p. 47.

Arthur Robson has been a member of The Theosophical Society for many years. He was born and educated in India and, after receiving his degree, taught in several schools in that country before coming to England to live in 1955. He has been active in the English Section of the Soceity since that time and has made a substantial contribution to theosophical literature. Among his major works are *Human Nature, Look At Your Karma, The Eternal Truths of Life*, and *Man and His Seven Principles*.

9.

COMPENSATION

Ralph Waldo Emerson

The wings of Time are black and white,
Pied with morning and with night.
Mountain tall and ocean deep
Trembling balance duly keep.
In changing moon, in tidal wave,
Glows the feud of Want and Have.
Gauge or more and less through space
Electric star and pencil plays.
The lonely Earth amid the balls
That hurry through the eternal halls,
A makeweight flying to the void,
Supplemental asteroid,
Or compensatory spark,
Shoots across the neutral Dark.

Man's the elm, and Wealth the vine,
Stanch and strong the tendrils twine:
Though the frail ringlets thee deceive,
None from its stock that vine can reave.
Fear not, then, thou child infirm,
There's no god dare wrong a worm.
Laurel crowns cleave to deserts
And powers to him who power exerts;
Hast not thy share? On winged feet,

Lo! it rushes thee to meet;
And all that Nature made thy own,
Floating in air or pent in stone,
Will rive the hills and swim the sea
And, like thy shadow, follow thee.

Ever since I was a boy I have wished to write a discourse on Compensation; for it seemed to me when very young that on this subject life was ahead of theology and the people knew more than the preachers taught. The documents too from which the doctrine is to be drawn, charmed my fancy by their endless variety, and lay, always before me, even in sleep; for they are the tools in our hands, the bread in our basket, the transactions of the street, the farm and the dwelling-house; greetings, relations, debts and credits, the influence of character, the nature and endowment of all men. It seemed to me also that in it might be shown men a ray of divinity, the present action of the soul of this world, clean from all vestige of tradition; and so the heart of man might be bathed by an inundation of eternal love, conversing with that which he knows was always and always must be, because it really is now. It appeared moreover that if this doctrine could be stated in terms with any resemblance to those bright intuitions in which this truth is sometimes revealed to us, it would be a star in many dark hours and crooked passages in our journey, that would not suffer us to lose our way.

I was lately confirmed in these desires by hearing a sermon at church. The preacher, a man esteemed for his orthodoxy, unfolded in the ordinary manner the doctrine of the Last Judgment. He assumed that judgment is not executed in this world; that the wicked are successful; that the good are miserable; and then urged from reason and from Scripture a compensation to be made to both parties in the next life. No offense appeared to be taken by the congregation at this doctrine. As far as I could observe when the meeting broke up they separated without remark on the sermon.

Yet what was the import of this teaching? What did the preacher mean by saying that the good are miserable in the present life? Was it that houses and lands, offices, wine, horses, dress, luxury, are had by unprincipled men, whilst the saints are poor and despised; and that a compensation is to be made to these last hereafter, by giving them the like gratifications another day, — bank-stock and doubloons, venison and champagne? This must be the compensation intended; for what else? Is it that they are to have leave to pray and praise? to love and serve men? Why, that they can do now. The legitimate inference the disciple would draw was, — 'We are to have *such* a good time as the sinners have now;' — or, to push it to its extreme import, — 'You sin now, we shall sin by and by; we would sin now, if we could; not being successful we expect our revenge tomorrow.'

The fallacy lay in the immense concession that the bad are successful; that justice is not done now. The blindness of the preacher consisted in deferring to the base estimate of the market of what constitutes a manly success, instead of confronting and convicting the world from the truth; announcing the presence of the soul; the omnipotence of the will; and so establishing the standard of good and ill, of success and falsehood.

I find a similar base tone in the popular religious works of the day and the same doctrines assumed by the literary men when occasionally they treat the related topics. I think that our popular theology has gained in decorum, and not in principle, over the superstitions it has displaced. *But men are better than their theology*. Their daily life gives it the lie. Every ingenuous and aspiring soul leaves the doctrine behind him in his own experience, and all men feel sometimes the falsehood which they cannot demonstrate. For men are wiser than they know. That which they hear in schools and pulpits without afterthought, if said in conversation would probably be questioned in silence. If a man dogmatize in a mixed company on Providence and the divine laws, he is answered by a silence which conveys well enough to an observer the dissatisfaction of the hearer, but his incapacity to make his own statement.

I shall attempt in this and the following chapter to record some facts that indicate the path of the law of Compensation; happy beyond my expectation if I shall truly draw the smallest arc of this circle.

Polarity, or action and reaction, we meet in every part of nature; in darkness and light; in heat and cold; in the ebb and flow of water; in male and female; in the inspiration and expiration of plants and animals; in the equation of quantity and quality in the fluids of the animal body; in the systole and diastole of the heart; in the undulations of fluids and of sound; in the centrifugal and centripetal gravity; in electricity, galvanism, and chemical affinity. Superinduce magnetism at one end of a needle, the opposite magnetism takes place at the other end. If the south attracts, the north repels. To empty here, you must condense there. An inevitable dualism bisects nature, so that each thing is a half, and suggests another thing to make it whole; as, spirit, matter; man, woman; odd, even; subjective, objective; in, out; upper, under; motion, rest; yea, nay.

Whilst the world is thus dual, so is every one of its parts. The entire system of things gets represented in every particle. There is somewhat that resembles the ebb and flow of the sea, day and night, man and woman, in a single needle of the pine, in a kernel of corn, in each individual of every animal tribe. The reaction, so grand in the elements, is repeated within these small boundaries. For example, in the animal kingdom the physiologist has observed that no creatures are favorites, but a certain compensation balances every gift and every defect. A surplusage given to one part is paid out of a reduction from another part of the same creature. If the head and neck are enlarged, the trunk and extremities are cut short.

The theory of the mechanic forces is another example. What we gain in power is lost in time, and the converse. The periodic or compensating errors of the planets is another instance. The influences of climate and soil in political history are another. The cold climate invigorates. The barren soil does not breed fevers, crocodiles, tigers or scorpions.

The same dualism underlies the nature and condition of man. Every excess causes a defect; every defect an excess. Every sweet hath its sour; every evil its good. Every faculty which is a receiver of pleasure has an equal penalty put on its abuse. It is to answer for its moderation with its life. For every grain of wit there is a grain of folly. For every thing you have missed, you have gained something else; and for every thing you gain, you lose something. If riches increase, they are increased that use them. If the gatherer gathers too much, Nature takes out of the man what she puts into his chest; swells the estate, but kills the owner. Nature hates monopolies and exceptions. The waves of the sea do not more speedily seek a level from their loftiest tossing than the varieties of condition tend to equalize themselves. There is always some leveling circumstance that puts down the overbearing, the strong, the rich, the fortunate, substantially on the same ground with all others. Is a man too strong and fierce for society and by temper and position a bad citizen, — a morose ruffian, with a dash of the pirate in him? — Nature sends him a troop of pretty sons and daughters who are getting along in the dame's classes at the village school, and love and fear for them smooth his grim scowl to courtesy. Thus she contrives to intenerate the granite and felspar, takes the boar out and puts the lamb in and keeps her balance true.

The farmer imagines power and place are fine things. But the President has paid dear for his White House. It has commonly cost him all his peace, and the best of his manly attributes. To preserve for a short time so conspicuous an appearance before the world, he is content to eat dust before the real masters who stand erect behind the throne. Or do men desire the more substantial and permanent grandeur of genius? Neither has this an immunity. He who by force of will or of thought is great and overlooks thousands, has the charges of that eminence. With every influx of light comes new danger. Has he light? he must bear witness to the light, and always outrun that sympathy which gives him such keen satisfaction, by his fidelity to new revelations of the incessant soul. He must hate father and mother, wife and child. Has he all that the world loves and admires and covets? — he must cast behind him their admiration, and afflict them by faithfulness to his truth, and become a byword and a hissing.

The law writes the laws of cities and nations. It is in vain to build or plot or combine against it. Things refuse to be mismanaged long. *Res nolunt diu male administrari.* Though no checks to a new evil appear, the checks exist, and will appear. If the government is cruel, the governor's life is not safe. If you tax too high, the revenue will yield nothing. If you make the criminal code sanguinary, juries will not convict. If the law is too mild, private vengeance comes in. If the government is a terrific democracy, the pressure is resisted by an over-charge of energy in the citizen, and life glows with a fiercer flame. The true life and satisfactions of man seem to elude the utmost rigors or felicities of condition and to establish themselves with great indifferency under all varieties of circumstances. Under the governments the influence of character remains the same, — in Turkey and in New England about alike. Under the primeval despots of Egypt, history honestly confesses that man must have been as free as culture could make him.

These appearances indicate the fact that the universe is represented in every one of its particles. Every thing in nature contains all the powers of nature. Every thing is made of one hidden stuff; as the naturalist sees one type under every metamorphosis, and regards a horse as a running man, a fish as a swimming man, a bird as a flying man, a tree as a rooted man. Each new form repeats not only the main character of the type, but part for part all the details, all the aims, furtherances, hindrances, energies and whole system of every other. Every occupation, trade, art, transaction, is a compend of the world and correlative of every other. Each one is an entire emblem of human life; of its good and ill, its trials, its enemies, its course and its end. And each one must somehow accommodate the whole man and recite all his destiny.

The world globes itself in a drop of dew. The microscope cannot find the animalcule which is less perfect for being little. Eyes, ears, taste, smell, motion, resistance, appetite, and organs of reproduction that take hold on eternity, — all find room to consist in the small creature. So do we put our life into every act. The true doctrine of omnipresence is that God reappears with all his parts in every moss and cobweb. The value of the universe contrives to throw itself into every point. If the good is there, so is the evil; if the affinity, so the repulsion; if the force, so the limitation.

Thus is the universe alive. All things are moral. That soul which within us is a sentiment, outside of us is a law. We feel its inspiration; out there in history we can see its fatal strength. "It is in the world, and the world was made by it." Justice is not postponed. A perfect equity adjusts its balance in all parts of life. Οἱ κύβοι Διὸς ἀεὶ εὐπίπτουσι, — The dice of God are always loaded. The world looks like a multiplication-table, or a mathematical equation, which, turn it how you will, balances itself. Take what figure you will, its exact value, nor more nor less, still returns to you. Every secret is told, every crime is punished, every virtue rewarded, every wrong redressed, in silence and certainty.

What we call retribution is the universal necessity by which the whole appears wherever a part appears. If you see smoke, there must be fire. If you see a hand or a limb, you know that the trunk to which it belongs is there behind.

Every act rewards itself, or in other words integrates itself, in a twofold manner; first in the thing, or in real nature; and secondly in the circumstance, or in apparent nature. Men call the circumstance the retribution. The causal retribution is in the thing and is seen by the soul. The retribution in the circumstance is seen by the understanding; it is inseparable from the thing, but is often spread over a long time and so does not become distinct until after many years. The specific stripes may follow late after the offense, but they follow because they accompany it. Crime and punishment grow out of one stem. Punishment is a fruit that unsuspected ripens within the flower of the pleasure which concealed it. Cause and effect, means and ends, seed and fruit, cannot be severed; for the effect already blooms in the cause, the end pre-exists in the means, the fruit in the seed.

Whilst thus the world will be whole and refuses to be disparted, we seek to act partially, to sunder, to appropriate; for example, — to gratify the senses we sever the pleasure of the sense from the needs of the character. The ingenuity of man has always been dedicated to the solution of one problem, — how to detach the sensual sweet, the sensual strong, the sensual bright, etc., from the moral sweet, the moral deep, the moral fair; that is, again,to contrive to cut clean off this upper surface so thin as to leave it bottomless; to get a *one end,* without an *other end.* The soul says, 'Eat'; the body would feast. The soul says, 'The man and woman shall be one flesh and one soul'; the body would join the flesh only. The soul says, 'Have dominion over all things to the ends of virtue'; the body would have the power over things to its own ends.

The soul strives amain to live and work through all things. It would be the only fact. All things shall be added unto it, — power, pleasure, knowledge, beauty. The particular man aims to be somebody; to set up for himself; to truck and higgle for a private good; and, in particulars, to ride that he may ride; to dress that he may be dressed; to eat that he may eat; and to govern, that he may be seen. Men seek to be great; they would have offices, wealth, power and fame. They think that to be great is to possess one side of nature, — the sweet, without the other side, the bitter.

This dividing and detaching is steadily counteracted. Up to this day it must be owned no projector has had the smallest success. The parted water reunites behind our hand. Pleasure is taken out of pleasant things, profit out of profitable things, power out of strong things, as soon as we seek to separate them from the whole. We can no more halve things and get the sensual good, by itself, than we can get an inside that shall have no outside, or a light without a shadow. "Drive out Nature with a fork, she comes running back."

Life invests itself with inevitable conditions, which the unwise seek to dodge, which one and another brags that he does not know, that they do not touch him; — but the brag is on his lips, the conditions are in his soul. If he escapes them in one part they attack him in another more vital part. If he has escaped them in form and in the appearance, it is because he has resisted his life and fled from himself, and the retribution is so much death. So signal is the failure of all attempts to make this separation of the good from the tax, that the experiment would not be tried, — since to try it is to be mad, — but for the circumstance that when the disease began in the will, of rebellion and separation, the intellect is at once infected, so that the man ceases to see God whole in each object, but is able to see the sensual allurement of an object and not see the sensual hurt; he sees the mermaid's head but not the dragon's tail, and thinks he can cut off that which he would have from that which he would not have. "How secret art thou who dwellest in the highest heavens in silence, O thou only great God, sprinkling with an unwearied providence certain penal blindless upon such as have unbridled desires!"[1]

The human soul is true to these facts in the painting of fable, of history, of law, of proverbs, of conversation. It finds a tongue in literature unawares. Thus the Greeks called Jupiter, Supreme Mind; but having traditionally ascribed to him many base actions, they involuntarily made amends to reason by tying up the hands of so bad a god. He is made as helpless as a king of England. Prometheus knows one secret which Jove must bargain for; Minerva, another. He cannot get his own thunders; Minerva keeps the key of them: —

Of all the gods, I only know the keys
That ope the solid doors within whose vaults
His thunders sleep.

A plain confession of the in-working of the All and of its moral aim. The Indian mythology ends in the same ethics; and it would seem impossible for any fable to be invented and get any currency which was not moral. Aurora forgot to ask youth for her lover, and though Tithonus is immortal, he is old. Achilles is not quite invulnerable; the sacred waters did not wash the heel by which Thetis held him. Siegfried, in the Nibelungen, is not quite immortal, for a leaf fell on his back whilst he was bathing in the dragon's blood, and that spot which it covered is mortal. And so it must be. There is a crack in every thing God has made. It would seem there is always this vindictive circumstance stealing in at unawares even into the wild poesy in which the human fancy attempted to make bold holiday and to shake itself free of the old laws, — this back-stroke, this kick of the gun, certifying that the law is fatal; that in nature nothing can be given, all things are sold.

This is that ancient doctrine of Nemesis, who keeps watch in the universe and lets no offense go unchastised. The Furies they said are attendants on justice, and if the sun in heaven should transgress his path they would punish him. The poets related that stone walls and iron swords and leathern thongs had an occult sympathy with the wrongs of their owners; that the belt which Ajax gave Hector dragged the Trojan hero over the field at the wheels of the car of Achilles, and the sword which Hector gave Ajax was that on whose point Ajax fell. They recorded that when the Thasians erected a statue to Theagenes, a victor in the games, one of his rivals went to it by night and endeavored to throw it down by repeated blows, until at last he moved it from its pedestal and was crushed to death beneath its fall.

This voice of fable has in it somewhat divine. It came from thought above the will of the writer. This is the best part of each writer which has nothing private in it; that which he does not know; that which flowed out of his constitution and not from his too active invention; that which in the study of a single artist you might not easily find, but in the study of many you would abstract as the spirit of them all. Phidias it is not, but the work of man in that early Hellenic world that I would know. The name and circumstance of Phidias, however convenient for history, embarrass when we come to the highest criticism. We are to see that which man was tending to do in a given period, and was hindered, or, if you will, modified in doing, by the interfering volitions of Phidias, of Dante, of Shakespeare, the organ whereby man at the moment wrought.

Still more striking is the expression of this fact in the proverbs of all nations, which are always the literature of reason, or the statements of an absolute truth without qualification. Proverbs, like the sacred books of each nation, are the sanctuary of the intuitions. That which the droning world, chained to appearances, will not allow the realist to say in his own words, it will suffer him to say in proverbs without contradiction. And this law of laws, which the pulpit, the senate and the college deny, is hourly preached in all markets and workshops by flights of proverbs, whose teaching is as true and as omnipresent as that of birds and flies.

All things are double, one against another. — Tit for tat; an eye for an eye; a tooth for a tooth; blood for blood; measure for measure; love for love. — Give, and it shall be given you. — He that watereth shall be watered himself. — What will you have? quoth God; pay for it and take it. — Nothing venture, nothing have. — Thou shalt be paid exactly for what thou hast done, no more, no less. — Who doth not work shall not eat. — Harm watch, harm catch. — Curses always recoil on the head of him who imprecates them. — If you put a chain around the neck of a slave, the other end fastens itself around your own. Bad counsel confounds the adviser. — The Devil is an ass.

It is thus written, because it is thus in life. Our action is overmastered and characterized above our will by the law of nature. We aim at a petty end quite aside from the public good, but our act arranges itself by irresistible magnetism in a line with the poles of the world.

A man cannot speak but he judges himself. With his will or against his will he draws his portrait to the eye of his companions by every word. Every opinion reacts on him who utters it. It is a thread-ball thrown at a mark, but the other end remains in the thrower's bag. Or rather it is a harpoon hurled at the whale, unwinding, as it flies, a coil of cord in the boat, and, if the harpoon is not good, or not well thrown, it will go nigh to cut the steersman in twain or to sink the boat. You cannot do wrong without suffering wrong. "No man had ever a point of pride that was not injurious to him," said Burke. The exclusive in fashionable life does not see that he excludes himself from enjoyment, in the attempt to appropriate it. The exclusionist in religion does not see that he shuts the door of heaven on himself, in striving to shut out others. Treat men as pawns and ninepins and you shall suffer as well as they. If you leave out their heart, you shall lose your own. The senses would make things of all persons; of women, of children, of the poor. The vulgar proverb, "I will get it from his purse or get it from his skin," is sound philosophy.

All infractions of love and equity in our social relations are speedily punished. They are punished by fear. Whilst I stand in simple relations to my fellow-man, I have no displeasure in meeting him. We meet as water meets water, or as two currents of air mix, with perfect diffusion and interpenetration of nature. But as soon as there is any departure from simplicity and attempt at halfness, or good for me that is not good for him, my neighbor feels the wrong; he shrinks from me as far as I have shrunk from him; his eyes no longer seek mine; there is war between us; there is hate in him and fear in me.

All the old abuses in society, universal and particular, all unjust accumulations of property and power, are avenged in the same manner. Fear is an instructor of great sagacity and the herald of all revolutions. One thing he teaches, that there is rottenness where he appears. He is a carrion crow, and though you see not well what he hovers for, there is death somewhere. Our property is timid, our laws are timid, our cultivated classes are timid. Fear for ages has boded and mowed and gibbered over government and property. That obscene bird is not there for nothing. He indicates great wrongs which must be revised.

Of the like nature is that expectation of change which instantly follows the suspension of our voluntary activity. The terror of cloudless noon, the emerald of Polycrates, the awe of prosperity, the instinct which leads every generous soul to impose on itself tasks of a noble asceticism and vicarious virtue, are the tremblings of the balance of justice through the heart and mind of man.

Experienced men of the world know very well that it is best to pay scot and lot as they go along, and that a man often pays dear for a small frugality. The borrower runs in his own debt. Has a man gained any thing who has received a hundred favors and rendered none? Has he gained by borrowing, through indolence or cunning, his neighbor's wares, or horses, or money? There arises on the deed the instant acknowledgement of benefit on the one part and of debt on the other; that is, of superiority and inferiority. The transaction remains in the memory of himself and his neighbor; and every new transaction alters according to its nature their relation to each other. He may soon come to see that he had better have broken his own bones than to have ridden in his neighbor's coach, and that "the highest price he can pay for a thing is to ask for it."

A wise man will extend this lesson to all parts of life, and know that it is the part of prudence to face every claimant and pay every just demand on your time, your talents, or your heart. Always pay; for first or last you must pay your entire debt. Persons and events may stand for a time between you and justice, but it is only a postponement. You must pay at last your own debt. If you are wise you will dread a prosperity which only loads you with more. Benefit is the end of nature. But for every benefit which you receive, a tax is levied. He is great who confers the most benefits. He is base, — and that is the one base thing in the universe, — to receive favors and render none. In the order of nature we cannot render benefits to those from whom we receive them, or only seldom. But the benefit we receive must be rendered again, line for line, deed for deed, cent for cent, to somebody. Beware of too much good staying in your hand. It will fast corrupt and worm worms. Pay it away quickly in some sort.

Labor is watched over by the same pitiless laws. Cheapest, say the prudent, is the dearest labor. What we buy in a broom, a mat, a wagon, a knife, is some application of good sense to a common want. It is best to pay in your land a skillful gardener, or to buy good sense applied to gardening; in your sailor, good sense applied to navigation; in the house, good sense applied to cooking, sewing, serving; in your agent, good sense applied to accounts and affairs. So do you multiply your presence, or spread yourself throughout your estate. But because of the dual constitution of things, in labor as in life there can be no cheating. The thief steals from himself. The swindler swindles himself. For the real price of labor is knowledge and virtue, whereof wealth and credit are signs. These signs, like paper money, may be counterfeited or stolen, but that which they represent, namely, knowledge and virtue, cannot be counterfeited or stolen. These ends of labor cannot be answered but by real exertions of the mind, and in obedience to pure motives. The cheat, the defaulter, the gambler, cannot extort the knowledge of material and moral nature which his honest care and pains yield to the operative. The law of nature is, Do the thing, and you shall have the power; but they who do not the thing have not the power.

Human labor, through all its forms, from the sharpening of a stake to the construction of a city or an epic, is one immense illustration of the perfect compensation of the universe. The absolute balance of Give and Take, the doctrine that every thing has its price, — and if that price is not paid, not that thing but something else is obtained, and that it is impossible to get any thing without its price, — is not less sublime in the columns of a ledger than in the budgets of states, in the laws of light and darkness, in all the action and reaction of nature. I cannot doubt that the high laws which each man sees implicated in those processes with which he is conversant, the stern ethics which sparkle on his chisel-edge, which are measured out by his plumb and foot-rule, which stand as manifest in the footing of the shop-bill as in the history of a state, — do recommend to him his trade, and though seldom named, exalt his business to his imagination.

The league between virtue and nature engages all things to assume a hostile front to vice. The beautiful laws and substances of the world persecute and whip the traitor. He finds that things are arranged for truth and benefit, but there is no den in the wide world to hide a rogue. Commit a crime, and the earth is made of glass. Commit a crime, and it seems as if a coat of snow fell on the ground, such as reveals in the woods the track of every partridge and fox and squirrel and mole. You cannot recall the spoken word, you cannot wipe out the foot-track, you cannot draw up the ladder, so as to leave no inlet or clew. Some damning circumstance always transpires. The laws and substances of nature, — water, snow, wind, gravitation, — becomes penalties to the thief.

On the other hand the law holds with equal sureness for all right action. Love, and you shall be loved. All love is mathematically just, as much as the two sides of an algebraic equation. The good man has absolute good, which like fire turns everything to its own nature, so that you cannot do him any harm; but as the royal armies sent against Napoleon, when he approached cast down their colors and from enemies became friends, so disasters of all kinds, as sickness, offence, poverty, prove benefactors: —

Winds blow and water roll
Strength to the brave and power and deity,
Yet in themselves are nothing.

The good are befriended even by weakness and defect. As no man had ever a point of pride that was not injurious to him, so no man had ever a defect that was not somewhere made useful to him. The stag in the fable admired his horns and blamed his feet, but when the hunter came, his feet saved him, and afterwards, caught in the thicket, his horns destroyed him. Every man in his lifetime needs to thank his faults. As no man thoroughly understands a truth until he has contended against it, so no man has a thorough acquaintance with the hindrances or talents of men until he has suffered from the one and seen the triumph of the other over his own want of the same. Has he a defect of temper that unfits him to live in society? Thereby he is driven to entertain himself alone and acquire habits of self-help; and thus, like the wounded oyster, he mends his shell with peal.

Our strength grows out of our weakness. The indignation which arms itself with secret forces does not awaken until we are pricked and stung and sorely assailed. A great man is always willing to be little. Whilst he sits on the cushion of advantages, he goes to sleep. When he is pushed, tormented, defeated, he has a chance to learn something; he has been put on his wits, on his manhood; he has gained facts; learns his ignorance; is cured of the insanity of conceit; has got moderation and real skill. The wise man throws himself on the side of his assailants. The would cicatrizes and falls off from him like a dead skin and when they would triumph, lo! he has passed on invulnerable. Blame is safer than praise. I hate to be defended in a newspaper. As long as all that is said is said against me, I feel a certain assurance of success. But as soon as honeyed words of praise are spoken for me I feel as one that lies unprotected before his enemies. In general, every evil to which we do not succumb is a benefactor. As the Sandwich Islander believes that the strength and valor of the enemy he kills passes into himself, so we gain the strength of the temptation we resist.

The same guards which protect us from disaster, defect and enmity, defend us, if we will, from selfishness and fraud. Bolts and bars are not the best of our institutions, nor is shrewdness in trade a mark of wisdom. Men suffer all their life long under the foolish superstition that they can be cheated. But it is as impossible for a man to be cheated by any one but himself, as for a thing to be and not to be at the same time. There is a third silent party to all our bargains. The nature and soul of things takes on itself the guaranty of the fulfillment of every contract, so that honest service cannot come to loss. If you serve an ungrateful master, serve him the more. Put God in your debt. Every stroke shall be repaid. The longer the payment is withholden, the better for you; for compound interest on compound interest is the rate and usage of this exchequer.

The history of persecution is a history of endeavors to cheat nature, to make water run uphill, to twist a rope of sand. It makes no difference whether the actors be many or one, a tyrant or a mob. A mob is a society of bodies voluntarily bereaving themselves of reason and traversing its work. The mob is man voluntarily descending to the nature of the beast. Its fit hour of activity is night. Its actions are insane, like its whole constitution. It persecutes a principle; it would whip a right; it would tar and feather justice, by inflicting fire and outrage upon the houses and persons of those who have these. It resembles the prank of boys, who run with fire-engines to put out the ruddy aurora streaming to the stars. The inviolate spirit turns their spite against the wrongdoers. The martyr cannot be dishonored. Every lash inflicted is a tongue of fame; every prison a more illustrious abode; every burned book or house enlightens the world; every suppressed or expunged word reverberates through the earth from side to side. Hours of sanity and consideration are always arriving to communities, as to individuals, when the truth is seen and the martyrs are justified.

Thus do all things preach the indifferency of circumstances. The man is all. Every thing has two sides, a good and an evil. Every advantage has its tax. I learn to be content. But the doctrine of compensation is not the doctrine of indifferency. The thoughtless say, on hearing these representations, — What boots it do well? there is one event to good and evil; if I gain any good I must pay for it; if I lose any good I gain some other; all actions are indifferent.

There is a deeper fact in the soul than compensation, to wit, its own nature. The soul is not a compensation, but a life. The soul *is*. Under all this running sea of circumstance, whose waters ebb and flow with perfect balance, lies the aboriginal abyss of real Being. Essence, or God, is not a relation or a part, but the whole. Being is the vast affirmative, excluding negation, self-balanced, and swallowing up all relations, parts and times within itself. Nature, truth, virtue, are the influx from thence. Vice is the absence or departure of the same. Nothing, Falsehood, may indeed stand as the great Night or shade on which as a background the living universe paints itself forth, but no fact is begotten by it; it cannot work, for it is not. It cannot work any good; it cannot work any harm. It is harm inasmuch as it is worse not to be than to be.

We feel defrauded of the retribution due to evil acts, because the criminal adheres to his vice and contumacy and does not come to a crisis or judgment anywhere in visible nature. There is no stunning confutation of his nonsense before men and angels. Has he therefore outwitted the law? Inasmuch as he carries the malignity and the lie with him he so far deceases from nature. In some manner there will be a demonstration of the wrong to the understanding also; but, should we not see it, this deadly deduction makes square the eternal account. Neither can it be said, on the other hand, that the gain of rectitude must be bought by any loss. There is no penalty to virtue; no penalty to wisdom; they are proper additions of being. In a virtuous action I properly *am;* in a virtuous act I add to the world; I plant into deserts conquered from Chaos and Nothing and see the darkness receding on the limits of the horizon. There can be no excess to love, none to knowledge, none to beauty, when these attributes are considered in the purest sense. The soul refuses limits, and always affirms an Optimism, never a Pessimism.

His life is a progress, and not a station, His instinct is trust. Our instinct uses "more" and "less" in application to man, of the *presence of the soul,* and not of its absence; the brave man is greater than the coward; the true, the benevolent, the wise, is more a man and not less, than the fool and knave. There is no tax on the good of virtue, for that is the incoming of God himself, or absolute existence, without any comparative. Material good has its tax, and if it came without desert or sweat, has no root in me, and the next sind will blow it away. But all the good of nature is the soul's, and may be had if paid for in nature's lawful coin, that is, by labor which the heart and the head allow. I no longer wish to meet a good I do not earn, for example to find a pot of buried gold, knowing that it brings with it new burdens. I do not wish more external goods, — neither possessions, nor honors, nor powers, nor persons. The gain is apparent; the tax is certain. But there is no tax on the knowledge that the compensation exists and that it is not desirable to dig up treasure. Herein I rejoice with a serene eternal peace. I contract the boundaries of possible mischief. I learn the wisdom of St. Bernard, — "Nothing can work me damage except myself; the harm that I sustain I carry about with me, and never am a real sufferer but by my own fault."

In the nature of the soul is the compensation for the inequalities of condition. The radical tragedy of nature seems to be the distinction of More and Less. How can Less not feel the pain; how not feel indignation or malevolence towards More? Look at those who have less faculty, and one feels sad and knows not well what to make of it. He almost shuns their eye; he fears they will upbraid God. What should they do? It seems a great injustice. But see the facts nearly and these mountainous inequalities vanish. Love reduces them as the sun melts the iceberg in the sea. The heart and soul of all men being one, this bitterness of *His* and *Mine* ceases. His is mine. I am my brother and my brother is me. If I feel overshadowed and outdone by great neighbors, I can yet love; I can still receive; and he that loveth maketh his own the grandeur he loves. Thereby I make the discovery that my brother is my guardian, acting for me with the friendliest designs, and the estate I so admired and envied is my own. It is the nature of the soul to appropriate all things. Jesus and Shakespeare are fragments of the soul, and by love I conquer and incorporate them in my own conscious domain. His virtue, — is not that mine? His wit, — if it cannot be made mine, it is not wit.

Such also is the natural history of calamity. The changes which break up at short intervals the prosperity of men are advertisements of a nature whose law is growth. Every soul is by this intrinsic necessity quitting its whole system of things, its friends and home and laws and faith, as the shellfish crawls out of its beautiful but stony case, because it no longer admits of its growth, and slowly forms a new house. In proportion to the vigor of the individual these revolutions are frequent, until in some happier mind they are incessant and all worldly relations hang very loosely about him, becoming as it were a transparent fluid membrane through which the living form is seen, and not, as in most men, an indurated heterogeneous fabric of many dates and of no settled character, in which the man is imprisoned. Then there can be enlargement, and the man of today scarcely recognizes the man of yesterday. And such should be the outward biography of man in time, a putting off of dead circumstances day by day, as he renews his raiment day by day. But to us, in our lapsed estate, resting, not advancing, resisting, not cooperating with the divine expansion, this growth comes by shocks.

We cannot part with our friends. We cannot let our angels go. We do not see that they only go out that archangels may come in. We are idolators of the old. We do not believe in the riches of the soul, in its proper eternity and omnipresence. We do not believe there is any force in today to rival or recreate that beautiful yesterday. We linger in the ruins of the old tent where once we had bread and shelter and organs, nor believe that the spirit can feed, cover, and nerve us again. We cannot again find aught so dear, so sweet, so graceful. But we sit and weep in vain. The voice of the Almighty saith, 'Up and onward for evermore!' We cannot stay amid the ruins. Neither will we rely on the new; and so we walk ever with reverted eyes, like those monsters who look backwards.

And yet the compensations of calamity are made apparent to the understanding also, after long intervals of time. A fever, a mutilation, a cruel disappointment, a loss of wealth, a loss of friends, seems at the moment unpaid loss, and unpayable. But the sure years reveal the deep remedial force that underlies all facts. The death of a dear friend, wife, brother, lover, which seemed nothing but privation, somewhat later assumes the aspect of a guide or genius; for it commonly operates revolutions in our way of life, terminates an epoch of infancy or of youth which was waiting to be closed, breaks up a wonted occupation, or a household, or style of living, and allows the formation of new ones more friendly to the growth of character. It permits or constrains the formation of new acquaintances and the reception of new influences that prove of the first importance to the next years; and the man or woman who would have remained a sunny garden-flower, with no room for its roots and too much sunshine for its head, by the falling of the walls and the neglect of the gardener is made the banyan of the forest, yielding shade and fruit to wide neighborhoods of men.

10.

IN THIS SILENCE, SANITY IS BORN

Karma as the Order of the Universe

George Koch

It may seem unsophisticated to say so, but it is important to realize at the outset what great privilege and opportunity is ours in being able to consciously study the mystery of karma, for most of us live most of our lives ignorant of both its existence and its workings. Having now awakened to it, however recently, we have before us the possibility of a fundamental transformation in the quality and nature of our lives. Here, in this mystery, lies the final sense and order of the universe, presenting itself in all forms, gross and subtle. Here, through this mystery, we may understand profoundly what it is to be one with life, to live in and with its order, to conduct our individual lives integrally in harmony with the one life manifesting through us.

Though the substance of Karma is a simple truth, its attainment may be a difficult and frustrating process, for the deeper we penetrate its mystery, the more unlike our preconceptions it becomes. Karma is but a word used to refer to a cosmic process, finally to *the* cosmic process that orders all things. It will without effort bear up under the closest and most penetrating inquiry, revealing to anyone sheath upon sheath of ever more subtle mystery, of ever more simple truth. The more penetrating the inquiry, the more unlike the initial understandings will the truth be. It is thus crucial that we not be led astray by our early openings into this mystery.

When we are first introduced to this great process it is likely that or perception will show it to be the law of action and reaction in human affairs. "As a man sows, so shall he reap" is the phrase which essentially embodies his view of Karma, and though this is a great truth in itself, deeper aspects remain yet to be uncovered. Karma, the superconscious process that teaches to man and woman the meaning of just and true action, is beyond this also the teacher of all mysteries. Karma, ultimately, is not merely a moral equalizer, but rather the very order of the universe itself; it moves within the spheres of justice and morality, but is not limited to them.

The contradictions that we come upon between our early understandings, profound and moving though they may have been at their time, and our later and more radical discoveries, are necessarily illusory. As the bud and the flower are vastly different, and yet quite the same, so are our early and later understandings of Karma seemingly in contradiction, yet truly harmonious.

If we seem then to wander into areas unfamiliar and without markings, let us be aware that what we witness cannot be confined by our early understandings, for it is behind and beyond all, is THAT from which all things spring. This is the great teacher, Karma, for being all things, it teaches all things, giving to each only what each is prepared to receive, without favor or dislike.

All morality, save the highest, is principled. To the most insecure, and therefore the most violent, the principle is simple and unwavering: survival at any cost. As education and civilization grow in a society, this one principle is modified, taking on nuances and exceptions. It widens into many areas of social intercourse, dictates dress and eating habits, governs what violence is acceptable and what is not. Men and women begin to become aware of the existence of principle, and morality and social justice take birth. Still, at the base of all this, hidden deep among the many philosophies, and simmering among the most noble of ideals and causes, the one principle continues to exist: survival. All social moralities, without exception, are modifications of this one base, and to a greater or lesser extent make it visible in their laws and social codes.

While it is important to see clearly the absolute rulership of this principle in all social morality, it would be a grave error to dismiss all such moralities as useless attempts at order and no more, for they surely are the first recognition of Karma by humanity, and though the perception is dim, yet it is there.

The early evolutionary consciousness, in its naturally confused and insecure awakening, has given rise to violence and social chaos; all about, nature demonstrates to this dim perception the vastness of its order: it shows in the regularity of its seasons, in the passing of day and night, in the cycles of the body and all living things in the absolute fulfillment of its laws that order exists. Within the chaos of human activity man tries to construct a parallel order, and with it to find a security, a protection from the chaos his unconscious has brought. Yet the imitation of order is not the same as order itself, and though man brings refinement upon refinement to his imitation, it is still made in chaos, and chaos it must contain. Not until the unconscious itself gives way can true order prevail. Through the imitation of order the one principle, survival, continues in all modifications.

Finally, the awareness dawns that at the same time as we attempt justice and morality through our laws and social codes, there is another justice at work, far beyond the artificial one that has been created, and quite real and uncompromising in its workings. The order man had dimly perceived around him is there within him as well, independent of any principle he might have constructed, and quite unconcerned with survival.

This order, which we call Karma, exists fully without principle, for principle, the movement for survival and its refinements, is but an artificial standard to which actions are self-consciously compared. Karma, being the order, the causeless, uncreated Principle and law itself, functions without reference or comparison, works as it does without imitation.

This is not a denial of the function of moral principle, for it has its rightful time in the scheme of things, but it is a recognition that the vast motion and order which lie behind and transcend us are not bound by our ideas and responses to them. In a wider sense of course, we too are this vast motion and order, and the chaos we speak of but a passing phantom, yet it is neither wise nor appropriate to confuse these different levels of understanding. Though we may give intellectual or emotional assent to the idea that all is in order, we must likewise know that what is truly order to one perception is just as truly chaos to another. It is only by understanding the chaos we see about us, and not by philosophically denying its existence, that we will finally reach the awareness of the wider truth that knows this chaos as order. Knowing all is in order and believing it are two quite different activities.

Already we have passed through four quite distinct perceptions of Karma: first, the confused and totally self-protective consciousness unaware of anything but threat; second, the beginning though dim perception of an order in the universe outside ourselves; third, the construction of an artificial order in an attempt to control the danger imposed by others equally insecure; and fourth, the recognition that independent of our artificial order there is another, vaster order, both beyond and including our activities, an order which functions free of principle, and by this freedom embodies the highest morality.

The implicit suggestion is that one can live without principle. It is at first blush a dangerous notion, for were it to be accepted without understanding, it could lead to great violence and social chaos, each doing what he or she pleased with little or no concern for the other. Yet, realistically, this is the state of affairs in which our world presently finds itself. It is not because our actions are without priciple that we are violent, but because our principles are born from our insecurity. Whether the principle is the basic one of survival, or a refinement of this in the form of religious dogma, political belief or social custom and law, the basically artificial nature of principled morality always and unavoidably ends in conflict and violence.

The discovery of fundamentally just and true action is not through any emotional or intellectual decision, not through any external or internal command or conceptualization, but rather only through a complete and free opening to the pure order which is in life itself; true morality is not an escape from life, not its imitation. It is life fulfilled, spontaneous, free to act as life requires, and not as dictated by idea or fear.

Having begun to realize the curious sensibility of this unprincipled morality, we come upon an inversion taking place in our lives. Our responsibility is no longer to live up to any principles, however noble, but rather solely to discover the law, the order and truth which are the highest morality. By committing ourselves to any theory or principle, we bind ourselves to our present ignorance, to our present disorder and artificiality.

The state of morality which is beyond principle is psychologically, spiritually free of time, and therefore a timebound process cannot lead to it. Yet there is value in the timebound process of living up to principles so long as one has not penetrated their artificial nature. Once this has been done, once it has been seen that principle is not order but an imitation of it, then to bind oneself so becomes a recessive, contrary action.

The existence of ungoverned morality has been known throughout time; it is spoken of in many ways by all of the esoteric mystical traditions, though references to it are often vague and superficially contradictory, even absurd. Yet this process is evident in many far quarters of the spiritual community, though it still as always remains rare. The movement through principles to an existence utterly free of them is "the gradual path to sudden awakening." One nurtures in oneself an intensification of principle and morality, a raptured attention to the problem of personal and world violence, a consequent deep devotion to one spiritual system or another as a means to resolve this violence. And then, opening like the first flower among many buds still closed and protected, one goes beyond the form of one's own spiritual quest, beyond teacher and religion, beyond obedience to principle and dictate; one become integrally free, integrally loving, moral and incapable of violence, quite unconcerned with survival. This is the marriage of mind and heart, itself rarely spoken of in the traditions, itself known as rarely as the individuals who manifest it.

This marriage is not a co-joining of the intellect and emotions, for these are to the true mind and heart what principled morality is to true morality; these are but shadows of the real existence, servants to it.

When attention is not present, but lost and drifting in the many fantasies of separative existence, relationships move quickly to misunderstanding and violence; here the emotions are called forth — anger or unhappiness follows. But these emotions are not things to be denied or controlled, for they are calling us to attention, calling us away from our heedless and unconscious drifting. When it is recognized that this is the true and natural function of emotion, then fear of and entrapment within it pass away naturally. With attention the need for this function is past. The cycles of elevation and depression end, and the true joy of existence is given room to manifest.

So too with the intellect, for while it is not capable of divining absolute truth, it may inquire sufficiently into the relative world to recognize the contradictions of relationship through principle. The intellect can penetrate to frustration, to the veil of vanity, but not beyond.

It is here, at the frustration of the intellect, with the attention called by the emotion, that the final failing of purely separative existence comes before the waiting consciousness. This consciousness, knowing fully and finally that it is both moral and stupid, incapable of living morally in its present state, becomes humble and silent. In this silence, sanity is born. What were once two separate activities, emotion and intellect, what once acted as sentiment and the acquisition of knowledge, now drop away, and but one existence remains. Here is is seen that no marriage has occurred, that the heart has not joined the mind, that no union has taken place because none was required; there is no separation. The mind and heart are one activity, often seen as two by virtue of the manifestation, but finally, beneath it all, one and only one, returned, fulfilled, the same one who began the perilous and unmarked journey, beyond ideas and ideals, unrestricted by principle and vow, ungoverned save by the very order which it is.

George Koch holds a Bachelor's degree in physics and has done graduate work in physics, education, and Eastern philosophy. He works as an engineering and media consultant in California, as well as writing and lecturing on various scientific and philosophical subjects. He was formerly President of the Los Angeles Branch of The Theosophical Society in America.

11.

KARMA IN MOTION

Felix Layton

Isaac Newton's Third Law of Motion states: "To every action there is an equal and opposite reaction." This is sometimes thought to be a statement of the Law of Karma. But Newton's three laws of motion consider only *physical* force, matter, and motion. Karma includes life, consciousness, and motive as well as physical force and matter. This article considers analogies between the limited laws of motion in the physical world and the all-inclusive principle of karma. It seeks by considering the laws of physical motion to gain increased understanding of the universal principle.

Imagine a large, heavy, steel ball at rest on a perfectly level plane. Imagine further that there is no friction between the ball and the plane. The ball will remain at rest until some force makes it move, but if it has once started to move it will continue to move indefinitely until something stops it. So said Sir Isaac Newton in his first Law of Motion, sometimes called the Law of Inertia, a law which has been verified countless times and seems to be common sense.

Now let a man somehow exert a force on this ball to push it in a certain direction. Let him continue to push the ball in the same direction for a long time. As long as he keeps pushing, the ball will move faster and faster. How fast it will finally move depends on how hard and how long the man pushes. This is according to Newton's second Law of Motion. Since this system is frictionless, when the man stops pushing, the ball continues to move in that direction.

Now suppose that the man who worked and pushed so hard, finds that he made a mistake and pushed the wrong way, and really wants the ball to go in the opposite direction! The ball now has "within it" the momentum which it stored when the man first pushed, and this momentum carries it steadily on in the direction of that first pushing in exact proportion to how hard and how long the man pushed — and if he pushed hard and long he will have to push exactly that amount in the opposite direction before he can stop the ball.

It all works out with absolute exactness. Knowledge of these laws is the basis for the calculations of forces to send space capsules on their way. Knowledge of the same laws enables men to calculate exactly what length of burn, generating a certain force, will slow, accelerate, or change direction a certain amount. One astronaut in flight remarked that we owe it all to Isaac Newton.

The laws seem to be absolute, and they apply not only to a single object and force but to any system of many masses and forces. Although first stated by Sir Isaac Newton they have been realities from the beginning of creation. They are part of the nature of things — or at least of the nature of force and matter.

Many people believe that there are correspondences between physical and spiritual laws. Let us first consider correspondences between these first two laws and wider fields.

The law of karma is often compared to Newton's third Law: "To every action there is an equal and opposite reaction," but perhaps even more interesting correspondences exist with the first two laws, and often those who quote the third law as an illustration of karma misunderstand Newton's meaning.

In laboratory experiments, and in the steel ball illustration two factors are involved: *force,* in the example, applied by the man pushing, and *matter,* in this case a steel ball. Let these two correspond to life and form or spirit and matter, or, in our illustration, to the unit of life or consciousness called a man linked to his bodies or personality represented by the steel ball. Let us assume that this life or consciousness functions *within* the body, or the steel ball, and not externally in the same way that the engine functions inside a car.

When such a unit of life, or consciousness, is starting its series of incarnations, it is attached to a body which as yet is at rest, like the ball, for no force has yet acted through it. The boundless level plane on which the ball can be pushed in any direction corresponds to nature, which will allow man to move in any direction he wants — if he works hard enough. As astronaut Eugene Cernan said, "Things may come with difficulty but nothing is impossible to man."

The unit of life, the man, looking out through the senses of the body, sees things he desires. This causes him to work, to strive to obtain them — to move toward them. Suppose he is attracted to wealth. He wants it. He works for it. He struggles and pushes toward it. Perhaps he does this for many lives. In doing so he is building an ever greater momentum in the direction of wealth, for nature gives go man that for which he works. When he obtains it however, he may find that it does not give him the happiness for which he had hoped. He ceases to push and strive toward the goal of wealth. He may continue to coast effortlessly, carried along by his past efforts, but his desires will soon be attracted to another goal and he will begin to try to move in a new direction. However, all his past effort over a long time has built a momentum in the direction of wealth and this keeps him moving in that direction until, after long struggle and pushing against circumstances which seem to frustrate his every effort to move in the new direction, he eventually stops the movement and is free to move in another direction. If this analogy holds, these forces are not merely equal to, they actually are the forces he himself has generated and is now opposing. The more strongly he struggles to stop the ball and move toward the new goal, the more violent will be his conflict with these forces of the past, but the sooner they will be overcome. A believer in karma would say that he is working out his karma.

The shifting of the individual's goal in life usually is toward a nobler goal and comes after some sort of "revelation" or expansion of consciousness. In the nature of things it is then that he tries to move in a new direction and meets the forces he generated earlier, which might be called his karma. Perhaps in this lies an explanation of the phrase, "Whom the Lord loveth he chasteneth." Men consider one whom the Lord loveth to be one who has seen a great goal, such as the service of mankind, and is struggling toward that. He is therefore probably facing momentum and forces he created when moving in other directions and struggling toward less noble goals. The struggle to overcome this momentum would be the chastening.

When an individual performs a "wrong" act, which causes pain to another, he does it only because he knows no better. It is not wrong for him. He is ignorant, as yet. If the karmic consequence of pain returned to him immediately he would probably resent it, fight against it, consider the world unfair to him. He would learn nothing and would probably make the same mistake again. If howeve, the Lords of Karma defer payment, so to speak, until he "changes direction" and then allow him to meet the consequences of his act, he may then be in a condition of mind which will enable him to learn from the experience of pain and replace the ignorance, which made him perform the wrong act, with wisdom which will prevent him from making that mistake again.

When a cannonball is shot from a cannon, the explosion causes a force to act on the ball and shoot it from the cannon's mouth. If this is the action, then the reaction of which Newton spoke is the force which pushes back on the cannon and causes it to recoil. His third law, applied to this case would mean that the force acting on the cannonball is equal to the force reacting on the cannon, and that they act in exactly opposite directions. This has an interesting correspondence, for just as the action of firing the shot cannot be performed without reaction on the cannon, so an individual in this world cannot perform an action which does not react on others. He must create karma with one or many others, or with the whole world, on whom his action produces an equal and opposite reaction. As with the gun, someone has to absorb the recoil. A man's acts may be of hate, of love, or mixtures of the two, but whatever they are they act and react, and these actions and reactions are always equal and opposite.

In this example of action which shoots the ball in one direction makes the gun recoil and this reaction or recoil is absorbed into the great mass of the earth, disturbing the whole earth's motion and equilibrium. The shock wave of big guns being fired can be felt to shake the ground at considerable distances, as the earth patiently absorbs the shocks. When the action has been performed, the earth's motion has been altered; it may have been accelerated, reduced, or pushed sideways. This alteration to the earth will be too small to measure but the motion of the ball may be very fast. Eventually the ball will hit the earth again and stop. When this happens it returns its energy to the earth; equilibrium is restored, for it exactly neutralizes the disturbance to the earth's motion, made when the gun was fired. The ball may be in the air for a relatively long or short time before it hits the ground, but eventually the disturbance to the earth's motion will be neutralized.

There are correspondences between this example and the law of karma which perhaps emphasize the reality of brotherhood for, whether we like it or not, everyone in the world is affected by every individual action as the whole world is affected by the firing of every gun. Let the firing of the cannon in the example correspond to an act performed by an individual. This greatly affects him as the explosion greatly affects the cannon ball, and it slightly affects the whole world. The condition of imbalance exists between the individual and the world until the karmic consequences are met as the ball hits the earth and equilibrium is restored.

The timing of the reaction is of crucial importance. When does this karmic reaction which restores equilibrium occur? There are references which suggest that at great sacrifice to those who perform the work, karmic consequences may be held back. The moment of impact of the cannon ball, which could be devastating to the individual, may be delayed until the individual is strong enough and in a condition to profit by facing such shocks. One such reference in *Light on the Path* says:

> . . . try to lift a little of the heavy karma of the world; give your aid to the few strong hands that hold back the powers of darkness from obtaining complete victory.[1]

It may well be that in the early stages of man's evolution, and probably today also, men are creating more karma of a destructive, painful type than of a constructive, helpful type. Perhaps in some way, at the cost of untold sacrifice, great Intelligences, Lords of Karma, take some of these ugly, painful forces and store them in their own consciousnesses until humanity and its individuals are ready and able to face them. When that time comes, their sacrifice will be over and the world, which could be overwhelmed if karmic settlements were promptly and automatically made, will literally have been saved. Perhaps such are the Lords of Karma and this is part of their function.

A later reference in *Light on the Path* describes a time when the individual reaches a stage where he can force the karmic consequences of his earlier selfish acts and take back the load which the Lords of Karma have been carrying for him. It suggests that there will now come a great clearing up and an opportunity for learning from this karma of the past as he does his part "to lift a little of the heavy karma of the world." Henceforth he will not be shielded but must face the full karmic consequences of his acts. The passage is an interesting reversal of the way the law of karma is usually stated:

> Out of the silence that is peace a resonant voice shall arise. And this voice will say: It is not well: thou hast reaped, now thou must sow. And knowing this voice to be the silence itself thou wilt obey.[2]

And what about karma-less-ness? It is said that when an individual completes his human pilgrimage he is no longer the slave of karma; he reaches a state of karma-less-ness. This happens, it is said, when his actions are completely selfless and his will (sublimated desires) is one with the One Will. Ordinary actions are self-centered and may be compared to the cannon ball flying within the earth's gravitational field. It is the self-centeredness which eventually draws the reaction back to the doer just as it is the earth's gravitational field which eventually draws the cannon ball back to earth. The completely unselfish action of the Adept, however, is not drawn back and neutralized. It might correspond to shooting a capsule into space which does not return and neutralize itself in earth impact. The laws, possibilities, and limitations of such selfless acts may correspond to completely different phenomena as the weightless world of space travel is completely different from our gravity-bound life on earth.

This article has considered only some details of karma. It has made no attempt to cover the whole sweep of the great law. The examples have been extremely simplified in order to make principles stand out. Only closed systems with two or three factors have been considered. Such simplification is used in early experiments in laboratories where students are learning to understand basic laws. The problems of engineering and physics, which they will study later, involve using these laws in complex open systems with many bodies, forces, actions and reactions, all interacting on one another. The painstaking application of the simple law to one part after another of the complex gives him the capacity to understand, balance, and control the resultants of such interconnected factors. Similarly, there may be principles considered in this article which can be used first to understand, and then to partially control the enormously complicated interacting systems of life which surround us with countless individuals, forces, actions, and reactions. Perhaps this article may suggest further correspondences. It seems a fruitful field. The correspondences have not been suggested as mere intellectual games but as ideas with practical yet spiritual significance.

References

1. Collins, Mabel, *Light on the Path,* Part I, Note to Rule 20.
2. Ibid., Part II, opening lines.

Felix Layton served from 1966 to 1972 as National Vice-President of The Theosophical Society in America, during which time he and Mrs. Layton were engaged in lecturing and organizing new groups for the study of Theosophy as part of the field expansion work of the Society. He was educated in England, Canada, and the United States, receiving the B.S. degree in physics at the University of Michigan and the M.A. degree at Stanford University. For a number of years he was active in educational work at the international Headquarters of The Theosophical Soceity in Adyar, Madras, India, serving as Principal of the Besant Theosophical School and, at a later period, as Principal of the Olcott Harijan Free Schools. He has traveled and lectured widely throughout India and other Asian countries, New Zealand, Australia, and Europe. He is the author of *Einstein's Theory in the Light of Theosophy*, and, with Mrs. Layton, of *Some Basic Concepts of Theosophy* and *Theosophy: Key to Understanding*.

12.

THE MEANING OF KARMA IN INTEGRAL PHILOSOPHY

Haridas Chaudhuri

Volumes have been written on the Law of Karma and its manifold ethico-religious implications as well as practical bearings upon human life and self-development. The purpose of this paper is to provide a brief account of the ultimate philosophical significance of the Law of Karma, especially in the light of Integralism;[1] the latest development in the Hindu-Buddhist tradition of India.

The fundamental concepts and principles of Integralism have been developed by the author from the teachings of Sri Aurobindo with necessary modifications suggested by the discoveries of modern science and psychology. In respect of its ontological root, it will be shown how the Law of Karma is a logical sequel to the integral world-view or comprehensive awareness of Being.

The major premise of integral philosophy may be spelled out in the form of the following ontological equation:

Being = Cosmic Energy = Entropy-
Negentrophy-Balance
Brahman = Mahashakti = Tamas-Rajas-Sattva

The meaning of the above question is that Being (ultimate reality or Brahman) is perfectly identical with, or rather non-different from (advaita), cosmic energy (Mahashakti), which is the fundamental energy of the cosmic whole.[2] The sign of equation is in this instance the mathematical symbol of the philosophical concept of nonduality. Nonduality means that we are dealing here not with two separate realities, but with one and the same reality endowed with two inseparable aspects and functions.

Cosmic energy is the basic energy of the cosmic whole from which endless diversities of empirical existence spring into being, in which they all abide, and into which they are dissolved again. The categories of our ordinary thought such as substance, antecedent linear cause, unity, plurality, etc., are inapplicable to the cosmic whole or fundamental energy. Such categories are developed in the human mind as practically useful tools of self-adjustment to the ever-changing environment. In consequence, their scope of application is strictly limited to finite empirical existents or observable phenomena, such as oceans and mountains, rivers and trees, animals and men, stars and galaxies. In so far then as cosmic energy itself is beyond the conceptual tools of intellect, it is incapable of further verbalization (nirguna, anirvachaniya). In respect of its essential being, it is the same as indefinable Being (nirguna Brahman).

Being is the externally self-existent and self-sufficient ground of the entire universe and its bewildering varieties of existence (namarupa). In so far as it is beyond the scope of application of such ordinary categories of human consciousness as space, time, unchanging substance, antecedent cause, etc., it is logically indeterminable (nirguna, nirakara). But so far as it is the creative source of the cosmic manifold, it is entirely nondifferent from cosmic energy. It is presumptuous on the part of the human mind to fathom the mystery of Being-Energy (Brahman-Shakti) by thoughtless application of such perceptual categories as space, time, substance, cause, etc.; or such metaphysical categories as matter and mind, nature and spirit; or such theological categories as body and soul, world and God, God and Satan; or such ethical categories as right and wrong, good and evil.

The Triune Structure of Cosmic Energy

The variegated universe in its primordial essence is then cosmic energy. Energy is the harmonious and dynamic unity of three inseparably interrelated forces. The dynamic interactions of these three interrelated modalities of energy give rise to all the fundamental laws of the universe governing our life and destiny. These forces are:

Material force	inertia	entropy	tamas	body
Vital force	activity	negentropy	rajas	life
Mental force	balance	syntropy	sattva	mind

The material force or physical energy is outward self-expression, space-time expansion, extroversion or gradual dissipation of energy. Traceable to this material aspect of energy is the recently discovered scientific truth that the universe in which we live is an expanding universe. Galaxies are tearing away from one another with tremendous speed, as it were, seized with some kind of cosmic hate or repulsion. In the process they are all losing energy little by little, slowly dissipating their life substance in an irretrievable manner. This is known in modern science as the Law of Entropy, the second law of thermodynamics.[3] The law applies not only to intergalactic relations, but to our human relations, too. The more we live an extroverted pattern of living, the more we dissipate our vital energies. The more we engage in the life style of fierce competition and hateful exclusion of one another, the more we squander our spiritual potential and tread the path of perdition. Herein we find the first important implication — the implication on the material level — of the Law of Karma. It is the ethical correlate, in the sphere of human relations, of the scientific Law of Entropy. As we live and act, so we enjoy or suffer, endure or die. The path of hate and exclusion is the path of gradual self-dissipation. The path of competition is the sure way to the abyss of annihilation.

The essence of the vital force (rajas, prana, elan) consists in inward self-gathering, self-centering, increasing self-organization and structural complexification. This gives rise to Nature's evolutionary process and man's historical order. The creative flow of evolution running through cosmic Nature is conditioned by increasing complexification of structure accompanied by corresponding simplification of function and behavior. The truth of this observation is exemplified even in such primordial energy structures as electrons, protons, atoms, molecules, cells, cellular societies, etc.

The one remarkable offshoot of this self-centering and self-structuring of energy is the creative emergence at critical moments of higher and higher qualities, functions, values and levels of being. For instance, when such divergent molecules as carbon, hydrogen, oxygen, nitrogen, etc., combine in definite proportions, a qualitative novelty, a unique and unprecedented modality of being, namely the living cell, is born. It shows the emergent ability for such new functions as spontaneous mobility, immanent growth from within, self-reparation, self-regulation, self-reproduction, etc. This is known in modern philosophy as the law of emergent or creative evolution. This law represents a higher synthesis in which the religious theory of creation out of nothing and the Darwinian theory of mechanistic evolution through natural selection are harmonized. In the course of evolution, new forms, new qualities, new values continually emerge into being.[4] Life evolved out of the abysmal depths of matter; animal sentience evolved out of the impetus of life; man's rational self-consciousness evolved out of the spiraling matrix of animal sentience. In the course of the creative advance of human evolution we know that god-like men, illumined persons endowed with cosmic truth-vision, evolve through prodigious centralization of consciousness. In yoga philosophy this is known as the Law of Tapas-Sristi. This means that when a person by virtue of long practice of intelligent and purposive self-organization (Brahmacharya) generates the internal psychic heat of creative spiritual energy (Tapas),[5] then new visions of truth, beauty, and perfection illuminate his mental horizon and transform his total being into a channel of creativity. Herein lies the secret of orginal creativity of all such masterminds as Buddha, Krishna, Christ, Moses, Mohammed, Zoroaster, Lao-tze, and the like.

According to a Hindu legend, at the beginning of a new cycle of creation, the creator Brahma was wondering what kind of fresh novelty he could produce this time. Suddenly he heard a voice from the void, declaring loud and clear: "Tapas, Tapas, Tapas," which means: "Go into the depth of your being, marshal all energy toward the center, and generate the internal heat of new creativity." It is this heat and flame of creativity which is variously known as the mystic fire, the splendor of inner lightening, the pure flame of divine love; the kundalini.

In our human life if we take to heart this principle of novel creation and develop a life style of self-centering and sincere dedication to some such supreme value as truth, beauty, goodness, perfection, peace, freedom and the like, then we are launched upon the path of increasing spiritual unfoldment. Self-development brings in an increasing measure the divine blessings of expanding knowledge, broadening compassion, intrinsic joy, and illumined action. We see here the law of Karma operative on the evolutionary level. Viewed from the evolutionary perspective, the law of karma may then be stated somewhat as follows:

> The more you intensify your consciousness in search of the true Self or the ultimate meaning of life, the more you gain access to unexpected treasures of the spirit.

The Law of Karma on the Cosmic Level

The inner evolutionary process eventually leads one to the cosmic vision of truth suffused with the sweetness of love and compassion. Revealed to the eye of cosmic vision is the essential structure of the cosmic whole as an all-encompassing, self-coherent system, which is self-adjusting, self-regulating and self-manifesting. Cosmic balance and harmony is the name of its essential form.

Viewed from different standpoints the cosmic balance acquires different names. When we look at it from the standpoint of intellect or reason, the cosmic balance appears as the rational structure of the universe or as the system of all systems. Herein lies the fundamental faith of the scientist and the philosopher. This faith consists, as Albert Einstein puts it, in "profound reverence for the rationality made manifest in existence." The more the scientist contemplates the operation of laws in nature, the more he is inspired with a religious attitude of awe and humility "towards the grandeur of reason incarnate in existence."[6]

It is by the way of developing the same attitude that the systems view[7] of the universe has evolved in contemporary scientific thought. From the philosophical viewpoint then the highest law of the universe, the supreme and eternal law (Dharma), appears as perfect self-consistency (Satyam). The world's various philosophical schools (darsanas) try to articulate this cosmic self-coherence in various conceptual frameworks.

The fundamental laws of science, such as the law of conservation of energy, and that of cause and effect, are expressions of the eternal Dharma on the scientific level. They may be said to constitute the intellectual aspect of the Law of Karma. In other words, from the intellectual standpoint, the Law of Karma means that nothing happens in this world without a definite cause. It follows that we can control any special kind of happening by suitably changing its cause. If for instance we know the cause of a particular kind of suffering, we can eliminate that suffering by rooting out its cause.

Viewed from the esthetic standpoint, the cosmic balance appears as the harmony of multitudinous sense-impressions. The human mind experiences this harmony of sensations as the beautiful (Sundaram). Since both the true and the beautiful are modes of expression of the spirit of harmony, they are certainly very akin to each other.

Viewed from the standpoint of volition and action, the universe as a self-coherent and self-adjusting system appears as an inviolable ethical order (Sivam). Our practical reason or moral sense perceives in the cosmic harmony an active principle of cosmic justice (Ritam, Bhadram, Subham) controlling the operations of Nature and the destinies of man.[8] Herein lies the specific meaning of the Law of Karma, as ordinarily understood — our faith in the moral structure of the universe. Moral faith can be formulated thus: as you sow, so you reap; like action, like consequence (jeman karma teman phal). Mahatma Gandhi laid special stress upon this implication of the Law of Karma:

violence begets violence, hatred begets hatred, so love alone can lift man from the self-destructive vicious circle of mutual negativity.

Another way the Law of Karma can be expressed is: "He who lives by the sword, perishes by the sword"; conversely, he who lives in the love of truth shines on the lotus of love. Whereas he who thrives on greed perishes in the mud, he who delights in self-giving for the good of others, receives the blessings of God in abundant measure.

In the biological sphere, the Law of Karma assumes the form of ecological balance. The quality of life degenerates if the proper balance is not maintained in the interrelationship of various life forms and in the interaction between life and the physical environment. Violation of this law in the shape of indiscriminate commercial exploitation of the precious resources of Nature has brought us today to the verge of serious ecological crisis. Mother Nature is warning us to the effect: control your greed, or perish.

In the sphere of international relations the Law of Karma is revealed in terms of the balance of power and justice. This means that military power should be employed in international politics only as a handmaid to international justice. Otherwise it is bound to prove self-destructive and internecine.

Unfortunately, at our present stage of evolution, there is a tragic divorce, a yawning chasm, between political power and ethical justice. Until and unless this gulf is bridged by bringing sanity into the sphere of political action the chances of abiding world peace are very slim indeed.

Thus it is the spirit of balance and harmony which sustains the universe in its proper course. Without the force of balance (sattva) holding sway over the opposite forces of tamas and rajas, matter and life, outward self-expansion and inward self-organization, the universe would cease to be the cosmic order that it is. It is the spirit of harmony that creatively holds together the disintegrating entropy of matter and the evolutionary negentropy of life. In consequence, the evolutionary process in man continuously advances toward higher and higher levels of consciousness — toward the heavenly boons of immortality (amiritam), truth, love and beauty (satyam, sivam, sundaram).

It is thus the law of harmony which constitutes the ultimate foundation of both science and religion. On the one hand it guarantees the conservation of all energy which is the cornerstone of science; on the other it guarantees the conservation of all values which is the cornerstone of ethics and religion. By harmonizing seemingly conflicting forces such as matter and life, nature and spirit, body and mind, existence and essence, fact and value, it provides the right kind of environment within which the process of creative evolution may go on and the precious fruits thereof be duly preserved.

On the cosmic scale, the spirit of balance (sattva) makes our universe a self-maintaining, self-adjusting, self-regulating system. Instead of an amorphous mass of chaos and confusion it is a self-coherent whole. This basic structural feature of the universe is personified in Hindu philosophy in the image of Lord Vishnu, the supreme God of harmony and love. He is associated with two seemingly conflicting symbols: the infinite serpent (Ananta) and the Sun-bird (Garuda).[9] This bears a striking resemblance to the image of Zarathustra whose two animal companions were, as Nietzsche points out, the serpent and the eagle. The serpent symbolizes the vital energy, the unconscious instinctual drive (libido), which has a tendency to dissipate itself in extroversion. But the same energy is also capable of being rechanneled in an entirely different direction — upward.

The sun-bird garuda is the symbol of the power of spirit. It is the spirit of freedom in upward evolution which transforms instinctual energy and carries it upward on the sunlit path toward the thousand-petalled blossoming of man's divine potential (Kundalini). This upward evolutionary movement is triggered by the ingathering and inwardly focussing concentration of consciousness (pratyahara, dharana and dhyana) oriented to the ultimate goal of life.

The Convergence of Science and Mysticism

It is an exciting development of our present time that modern science, as a result of its recent revolutionary discoveries, has come very close to the eternal truths of mysticism. Contemporary science, following the lead of Einstein and Planck, has rejected the atomistic, mechanistic, and reductionistic outlook of older scientists. It is developing a systemic world view of enormous significance. Implicit in this development is a perfect reversal of outlook revealing the cosmic manifold as the diversification of one unified field of energy.

Bringing together the laws of science and the truths of mysticism, Integral Philosophy contemplates the cosmic whole as a superorganic unity and self-harmonizing system of divergent forces imperceptibly jostling and blending with one another within the limits of an all-controlling order (eternal dharma). Integral Yoga, which is the practical application of the integral world view, lays its major emphasis upon the need for total integration of personality with a view to perfecting the art of harmonious living in tune with the creative urge of Being (Brahman).[10]

Let us now turn to a brief consideration of the implication of the law of karma in regard to the trend of human self-development. Man holds in the depth of his being a profound spiritual potential, a divine spark for endless perfectibility. This is his *swadharma,* his distinctive human essence. The law of cosmic balance (viswa dharma) that we mentioned before maintains the dynamic and evolutionary balance of life by harmonizing opposite forces such as matter and life, devolution and evolution, regress and progress. In our human life the two most fundamental dynamic forces are *karma* and *swadharma,* the conative thrust of the past and the developmental attraction of the future, the drive of desire embodied in samskara and the dream of self-perfection embodied in spiritual aspiration (aspriha, sankalpa).

In other words, all our dynamic thinking oriented to the future is the result of constant interaction between the forces of the past and the future, between *karma* and *swadharma,* between samskara and sankalpa, between the will to live and enjoy, and the will to love and be one with Being. To put it in still other words, the dynamics of our self-unfoldment are the result of active interplay between the unseen force of past actions (adrista) and the free initiative for higher development (purusakara), between the force of past history and the light of potential liberation (moksa).

The more our knowledge expands, the more we learn to make a judicious adjustment between the karmic dynamism of the past and the creative urge of our inner potential oriented to the future. The motivations flowing from such interaction ultimately determine our course of evolution.

Be it noted here in passing that Karma does not mean any external coercive agency. It does not mean the kind of supernatural fate which was illustrated in the tragic dramas of the ancient Greeks. Nor does it mean any arbitrary fiat or predetermined command of the divine will (kismet). That would be a violation of the ethical order of life (Ritam) which the Law of Karma presupposes.

Be it also noted that true freedom does not mean absolutely arbitrary action or irrational choice which some modern existentialist philosophers eulogize. Rightly understood, freedom means our ability to act and live in the light of our own human essence (swadharma), the inner light revealing the purpose of our being as a unique mode of manifestation of Being, a distinctive creative center of the cosmic whole (Brahman, Purnam).

In an attempt to actualize the spiritual potential, some mystics aspire for immortality after death on the supernatural plane. If they follow the right path, they surely can attain such supernatural self-fulfillment. The Bhakti Yoga tradition of India,[11] as well as the currents of devotional mysticism flowing through Judaism, Christianity and Sufism, emphasize this Karmic connection between authentic divine love and rapturous communion with God, the supernatural Lord of the universe.

Some spiritual seekers focus the deep longing of their hearts upon blissful union with transcendent Being, the eternal Spirit or indeterminable Godhead beyond God. This is especially emphasized in the contemplative approach of the Yoga of Knowledge in India,[12] and in the mystical traditions of Plato and Plotinus, Jacob Boehme and Meister Eckhart, Jalal Uddin Rumi and pseudo-Dionysius and others.

It should be noted here that the Theosophical Movement has rendered a signal service to sincere spiritual seekers all over the world by laying stress upon the validity of all the major religious and spiritual paths as means of ultimate spiritual fulfillment.

Integral Yoga shares with Theosophy this universality of spiritual outlook. Its special emphasis is geared to the evolutionary potentials of the emerging New Age — the Supramental Age. A suitable integration of the future-oriented spiritual values in the world's major mystical traditions is the dominant keynote of this new yoga dedicated to the outflowering of the Divine in global humanity.

The Karmic significance of Integral Yoga is that if we learn how to consciously cooperate with the creative force of planetary evolution as it is shaping up with the passage of time, mankind's age-old dream of the kingdom of heaven on earth., i.e., an internationally unified world order controlled by the power of truth, justice and love, can inevitably come true.

So the focus of integral self-discipline does not lie on mystic self-realization, whether on the supernatural level or on the transcendental level. Its focus is rather on the paramount desirability of harmonizing the mystic realization with the evolutionary perspective as well as the individuated self-discovery. United with the eternal, the integrated individual would joyfully cooperate with the process of evolution toward the emergence of a new global society.[13]

References

[1] Haridas Chaudhuri, *Being, Evolution & Imortality*. Wheaton, Illinois: Quest Books, 1974.

[2] Ibid, Ch. VII.

[3]. Isaac Asimov, *The New Intelligent Man's Guide to Science*. New York: Basic Books, 1965, p. 328.

[4] Samuel Alexander, *Space, Time, and Deity*. Vol. I. London: George Allen & Unwin.

[5] S. Radhakrishnan, *The Principal Upanishads*. New York: Harper, 1953. p. 253-54.

[6] Albert Einstein, *Out of My Later Years*. New York: Wisdom Library, a division of Philosophical Library, 1950. P. 33.

[7] Ervin Laszlo, *The Systems View of the World*. New York: George Braziller, 1972.

[8] S. Chatterjee & Datta, *An Introduction to Indian Philosophy*. Calcutta: University of Calcutta, 1950. p. 14-15.

[9] Heinrich Zimmer, *Myths and Symbols in Indian Art & Civilization.* New York: Pantheon Books, 1947. p. 76.

[10] Haridas Chaudhuri, *Integral Yoga: The Concept of Harmonious and Creative Living.* Wheaton, Illinois: Quest Books, 1974. Ch. 1.

[11] Ibid., pp. 67-71.

[12] Ibid., pp. 62-66.

[13] Ibid, pp. 51-52, 81-82.

Haridas Chaudhuri was Professor of Philosophy and President of the California Institute of Asian Studies in San Francisco. He also served as President of the Cultural Integration Fellowship, a group dedicated to the promotion of cultural understanding between East and West. He received his doctorate in philosophy from the University of Calcutta in 1947 and, before coming to the United States, he was a member of the educational service of the government of West Bengal and Chairman of the Department of Philosophy at Krishnagar College. He is the author of the Quest Books *Integral Yoga, Being, Evolutaion and Immortality,* and *The Evolution of Integral Consciousness.*

13.

THE SIDE BLOWS OF KARMA

Some Thoughts on the Outworking of Karma

George E. Linton

> "... you know nothing of the *ins* and outs of the work of Karma — of the 'side blows' of this terrible law."[1]

The quotation is from a letter to Mr. A. P. Sinnett, received by him in London in 1884, from the Mahatma Koot Hoomi. The Mahatma is discussing with Sinnett the failure of an endeavor to establish in India a newspaper under the latter's management. The previous year, the owners of the Allahabad *Pioneer* had terminated Sinnett's editorship of that paper, and he and his friends had been endeavoring to raise sufficient funds from the Indians to start a new paper which would be sympathetic to the Indian viewpoint. The endeavor had failed, due to the lack of support by the Indian financiers. The Mahatma asks Sinnett if he ever had any idea as to the *real reason* why the venture had failed, and then he intimates that it was a karmic "side blow" occasioned by the fact that in his earlier years in India, Sinnett had looked upon the Indians as an inferior race and had felt a profound contempt for them at that time. So at this later date, when he wanted to help the Indians and could have done much useful work for their betterment, his past karma denied him the opportunity.

The short study which follows is an endeavor to consider some of the ways in which karma appears to operate, based on information which is available, together with some added observations. Many events occur which to our limited observation are seemingly accidental or without adequate explanation; some are pleasant and some are tragic. Yet if we could see the entire picture, we would probably find that they are all the direct or indirect results of past actions, emotions, or thoughts. Take for example the large number of fatalities that occur each year on our highways. From a superficial point of view, there appears to be no logical moral reason why a particular accident occurs at a particular time and place, involving certain specific individuals. There is no apparent reason why "X" should be the one to run into "Y", a total stranger, and kill him. But perhaps they are not such total strangers as it appears at first thought. This is where the theory of reincarnation comes into the picture and adds the missing parts of the story which enable one to see that there may be some link that will explain the reason for this particular "accident." Perhaps the two entities who are the real beings who are at the present time functioning on the physical plane as "X" and "Y" have met before, in some previous incarnation; perhaps "X" is settling some past action in which "Y" has been involved and has to account for. But whatever the reason, there must have been some antecedent cause for the occurrence if one is to believe in a moral law of universal justice operating in the world. To the occultist, nothing can happen by accident.

Or again, some chance meeting may bring about a life-long friendship or some other good fortune for no apparent reason. Again appearance may be deceiving, and what appears to be accidental may be really the fulfillment of some cause set in motion earlier.

First, perhaps it would be advisable to review briefly the general concept of the law of karma and how it operates. A general outline can be found in many theosophical books, so there is no need to discuss the subject at length here, but a few basic considerations may be helpful. It is considered to be a basic law in nature that when equilibrium is disturbed at any point, a corrective action must take place sooner or later to restore the balance. Since manifestation itself is an action that disturbs the equilibrium of matter in *pralaya* (the state of rest in which exists during periods of inactivity), nature is ever in the process of restoring balances, hence it is stated that karma is action (implying also reaction). Ceaseless eternal motion is the order of the universe, states one of the Mahatmas in a letter to Mr. Sinnett, and affinity or attraction its handmaid of all work.[2]

If karma is a universal law in nature, its operation should and must follow (ultimately) a lawful pattern, and therefore if all the facts regarding a relationship are known it should be possible to accurately predict the results that will follow. In other words, a proper understanding of the law of cause and effect at all levels of being should enable one so to order his life that certain definite results will ensue. In general, however, few people stop to consider the underlying causes of many of the things that happen to them, being content to attribute these to circumstances, chance, or fate. They are content to deal with results rather than to seek for basic causes and deal with these causes. Life in the western world today is so busy and hectic that few take the necessary time to analyze things and find out the why of them. In fact, few would be willing to admit that they are living and operating within moral and spiritual energy fields, the laws governing which are as unerring, impersonal, and predictable as the laws governing the gravitational and electromagnetic fields. Many in fact would be loath to acknowledge that everything that happens to them is the result of actions which they themselves have set in motion at sometime in the past, either in this or in some prior incarnation.

A recognition of the existence of such moral and ethical laws and a search for knowledge as to how best to live in accordance with them would go far toward making life more livable and would enable mankind to progress more swiftly along its evolutionary path. Instead we are content to spend much of our time and energy trying to counter effects without seeking to find the underlying causes, thus bringing upon ourselves much unnecessary trouble, as for instance when we get an acid stomach, we seek to overcome the difficulty by taking some patent medicine, rather than finding out what is wrong with our eating habits and correcting them. Or, again, we raise our taxes in order to provide treatment and care for chronic alcoholics, while at the same time spending uncounted millions of dollars promoting the sale of alcoholic beverages, thus encouraging people to become alcoholics.

The concept of a universal law of justice is a simple one in principle. It is only when we begin to apply it to specific situations that we begin to have difficulty in observing its operation. Comprehension requires an understanding of basic theosophic concepts regarding the planes of nature, the origin and purpose of life, the total constitution of man and his various vehicles of consciousness. Unless one has an understanding of the fact that man is essentially a spiritual being, rooted in an ultimate reality and expressing himself on the mental, emotional, and physical planes of nature in vehicles suitable for use on those planes throughout a long series of incarnations in these different vestures of evolutionary experiencing, one will be unable to realize that nature has laws which are operative at these higher levels with as great a degree of certainty as those which are known at the physical level. Without this knowledge of the total picture of man, the idea of karmic law will be difficult to comprehend.

According to Dr. Annie Besant, every event in or lives, at whatever level, is linked to a preceding cause, and generally also to a succeeding result, so that life appears to us to be a continuous flow of events.[3]

In many instances we can perceive, or imagine that we can, the direct action of this law of compensation or balance as it applies to an individual person, provided the balancing effect takes place within a short period of time. If the karma has been accumulated at some earlier time in the life of the person or in some previous incarnation, we are normally unable to make any reasonable connection with the current event, since the whole picture is not available to us in the ordinary conditions of consciousness; but this lack of knowledge does not preclude the existence of the chain of causative events. We are constantly in the process of generating new karma, or balancing up past actions, and the results we think of in terms of good or bad, helpful or harmful, etc. Of course, in reality there is neither good nor bad karma since these are relative terms coined by man to describe things on the basis of his own judgment. Karma in itself is without attributes of man-made morality.

The intricate network of events impinging upon an individual and producing an offsetting reaction in him might be illustrated graphically by analogy to the vector diagrams used in the analysis of mechanical forces in the study of mechanics. In these diagrams the direction of the force is indicated by the direction of the line and the strength of the force by its relative length. The composite action of a group of forces acting through a given point produces a resultant which is of a certain strength and direction. To produce a state of equilibrium, another force equal and opposite to this resultant must be applied. The analogy fits quite well if we consider the individual as the point and the external forces acting upon him from differing directions as the vectors, producing a resultant effect which we call his karma. To maintain his state of equilibrium, he must exert a force which will neutralize the external forces, otherwise he will be pushed about by them until he, willingly or unwillingly, does something to bring about the balance, i.e., until he has settled the karmic debt.

Karma can be considered under several categories such as personal karma and group karma (national, racial, religious, etc.), or by levels of causation and outworking, or by time sequence. By this last is meant such things as current, earlier in life, or in some past incarnation. It is said that karma which has been accumulated in past incarnations is apportioned to the individual in a particular lifetime by certain intelligent forces in nature (generally referred to as the *Lipika*). The special function of these forces seems to be that of maintaining the integral balance of the universe and therefore of all the separate elements within it. The methods by which this is accomplished are not easily comprehended, except possibly by those who would personalize these forces as agents of an anthropomorphic God.

It is stated by stome students that no one is burdened in any one lifetime with an amount of his past karma greater than he is able to bear. Some persons might question this assurance when all the "slings and arrows of outrageous fortune" that are heaped upon them seem to be too much for them to cope with; but somehow most people do seem to manage to get through life, even though it isn't always easy. This applies especially to those circumstances which appear to be mostly burdens and misfortunes. Whether or not people have the same capacity to bear excessive good fortune might be questioned, as persons in these circumstances are the ones who seem to fail most often to make the best use of their opportunities. Few indeed seem to be able to withstand the effects of excessive wealth or power without abusing the opportunities and obligations that these offer or require, and thus creating for themselves much new karma of an unfortunate kind that they will be long in working out. As one of the Indian Adepts once remarked to Mr. Sinnett, "It is only in adversity that we can discover the true man." History seems to bear out this statement as excessive affluence, either individually or as a nation, is usually followed in a short time by decadence.

If we consider how karma works at the superphysical levels of consciousness, we need to understand how thought and emotion act and react in our lives. The matter of these planes being much more tenuous and rapid in movement than that of the dense physical, it is natural to expect that actions and reactions will occur with greater suddenness and rapidity at those levels. Tensions and disturbances in the emotional and mental planes can discharge themselves suddenly and without violence, as can an electrical discharge or the elements in a thunderstorm.

When the psychic atmosphere thus erupts, we see the results often in physical form, whether natural or man-made as in the case of revolutions, mob violence, or political disturbances. When a group of people or a nation builds up vast clouds of turbulence in the psychic atmosphere, it can seldom be dissipated slowly, but generally takes the form of physical disruption and violence such as we are now witnessing in connection with racial and social problems.

The mechanics by which karmic obligations are carried forward from one incarnation to the next until they are balanced out is something that is not easy to comprehend. During the intermediate periods between incarnations, the experiences of the incarnation just completed are said to be assimilated into the Ego or spiritual nature by a process analagous to digestion, and the valuable parts of such experiences are built into the causal body, the permanent vehicle of the individual consciousness on the plane of abstract mnd. The portions not suitable for absorption in the form of traits of character, capacities, talents, etc., are said to be left behind at the threshold of the heaven world, to be picked up again by the entity when it returns to incarnation at the physical level. The amount of this carry-over of unfinished business must be considerable, with humanity still at the present stage of imperfection, and so we can probably attribute many things in our lives to actions that we ourselves have generated in prior incarnations. The actual method by which these uncompleted actions (primarily of a less spiritual nature) are brought forward from incarnation to incarnation is not described in theosophical literature except in general terms, and this mostly by analogy. It is indicated that the individuality through the causal body maintains a continuing connection with the lower planes through attachments to certain particular "atoms" of those planes which perform the function of supplying vibratory or harmonic capabilities around which it attracts matter of the lower planes when reincarnating. These "atoms" collect the matter of the astral and physical planes suitable to the requirements of the individuality according to karmic law.

In Buddhist metaphysics, it is stated that the skandhas play an important part in the transmission of the "unfinished business" of one incarnation to the next. The skandhas are said to be the elements of limited existence, the "bundles of attributes" of the personal self, which are ever at work preparing the abstract mold, or "privation" of the future "new being."[4] In Buddhist philosophy these are listed as five in number, and together they make up the personal self with its sense of separate existence. While they disappear at time of death, they form the attributes of the future personality, and although there is no personal recollection of them in the new brain-mind in the ensuing incarnation, nevertheless they appear to be "forwarders" of the results of past action, in part at least. Thus when the individual returns again to the sphere of objective existence, part of the karma embodied in these privations is assumed in the new life (incarnation). The remainder presumably carries over until a still later incarnation. Perhaps we may infer that the "abstract mold" referred to attracts to itself matter of the lower planes that is harmonically attuned to its vibratory rates, and thus we get the type of physical, etheric, and emotional bodies which we deserve and to which we are entitled. "Like attracts like" as we all know, and this should be as applicable to the mental and emotional worlds as it is to the physical. The Mahatma, in another of his letters to Mr. Sinnett, asserts that "this law of attraction assersts itself in many seemingly inexplicable incidents in life, into which the entity has been drawn by the preponderating influences of past life actions."[5]

It is indicated by a number of clairvoyant investigators that the outline or characteristics of both the mental and emotional bodies are formed by or for the returning entity prior to the formation of the etheric and dense physical bodies for the projected incarnation. From this it would seem that the course the personality is to take in a particular incarnation is determined to a large extent prior to the birth of the physical body. Some investigators have indicated that some of the specific elements of this coloring process enter into the aura of the child at an early age and become diffused into the aura at the astral and lower levels. Possibly this is part of the method of operation of the skandhas of the Buddhists. The Mahtma writing to Mr. Sinnett further corroborates this point when he states that there are no "accidents of birth," as the new personality coming into incarnation is almost entirely the product of the past, and that the circumstances of the new existence have already been determined essentially by ourselves, meaning presumably our higher or spiritual selves. The cholera victim, he says, could not have died from the disease had not the "germs" for the development of the disease existed within him from birth. It would seem that the word "germs" is used here in the sense of latent causes rather than in the medical sense.

In considering further some of the ways in which karma works, it is said that physical acts to another produce reactions of a physical nature, depending in type and effect upon the motive behind the act as well as the act itself. Generosity from an unselfish motive is said to be productive of an agreeable environment in the future, whereas the same act performed from a selfish motive will not produce the same result as regards the future circumstances. Mistaken efforts to help another, performed from a good motive, will produce less reaction than if done from a poor motive, but in either case, the balance of justice must eventually be restored.[6] Deliberate cruelty, whether to man or animal, is said to result in physical impairment of some appropriate kind in a later incarnation. A person suffering from some congenital handicap or crippling disease may wonder why fate has visited such affliction on him for no reason of which he is aware in his own mind., i.e., his present brain consciousness. But perhaps if he could see behind the veil, and gain a more comprehensive view of things, he would see that he is only paying a just debt for something that he has done in some earlier incarnation. At the level of consciousness of the spiritual self, the individual is undoubtedly aware of the reasons for the presently existing situation.

Most every investigator capable of observing at the level of consciousness of the immortal self, and who can trace back the life of an entity though past incarnations, has testified that deliberate cruelty is one of the most terrible of crimes and results in the most severe karmic repayments. Some of these investigators indicate that this situation applies not alone to actions between man and man but also to man's treatment of the animal kingdom. Unintentional cruelty or cruelty from necessity do not appear to evoke the drastic karmic responses that accrue from intentional cruelty. It may be a long time before the world is free from pain and suffering, but to deliberately add to the existing accumulation is not aiding in the evolution of life on our planet.

Before leaving this point, it should be recognized that curelty to another human being can be perpetrated at the mental and emotional levels as well as at the physical level. In fact it seems probable that some people generate more suffering and anguish among their families and friends in this manner than by physical means, and oftentimes are quite unaware of it. But regardless of the manner in which the cruelty is manifested, whether intentional or not, the law of compensation will eventually bring about suitable redress.

Neither should we overlook the other side of the ledger, since love as well as hate is a binding force; while its reactions may be much more agreeable to bear, it is still something which binds people together. As to whether this type of link is a help or a hindrance to one's evoutionary advancement is perhaps a matter for individual consideration. Both are creators od karmic ties, and eventually it would seem that a time must come in one's stage of evolution when one should not be bound by either. Action without desire for the results of the action has ever been the attitude of the seeker after liberation from the bondage of the personal self, an attitude ably set forth in the Hindu classic, the *Bhagavad Gita.*

The collective karma of a group or a nation is something to which we probably give much less thought than to our individual karma. This is perhaps due in part to the fact that it is less observable and not as easily understood as our personal situation. The greater the freedom of the individual and the better the educational level, the greater the opportunity to become involved with the larger units of society and thus participate in the collective karma of the nation or group. In times past, when communication was limited — and even in some underdeveloped countries today — interest was and is centered more at the family and group level, and probably the collective karma was much less than in the Western nations of the world today with the worldwide contacts, communication, business problems, and political differences which exist. A public generally enlightened about events on a global scale, with all the problems involved between nations and cultures, must be creating a vast amount of collective karma, not only physically but also emotionally and mentally. Moral and ethical conduct by a nation becomes more and more a responsibility of the individuals in that nation. Considering the violent thoughts and feelings, mostly of a negative kind, which are being aroused both within the nations and on a global scale, the psychic atmosphere of the world today must be full of turbulence and charged to the point of explosiveness. It is little wonder that we are witnessing so much violence and turmoil.

The Christian scripture admonishes us to return good for evil, and while this evokes the heart qualities in man, it still leaves him tied karmically to the recipient of his meritorious action. Return good for good, for evil, justice, says the Confucian, which would seem to be more in keeping with a philosophical approach to life. This approach would also seem to be more in keeping with the teachings of the Lord Krishna as given in the *Bhagavad Gita,* where a more impersonal attitude toward the results of one's actions is advised.

Justice "makes no difference between the many and the few," says the previously quoted Mahatma,[7] which would seem to indicate that the integrity of a nation or a social group is just as important as one's personal integrity, and that all alike are weighed in the scales of justice. But how often do we find complete honesty and true integrity in the field of international diplomacy, or even in the business world? It would seem that the individual citizen should be as much concerned with the honesty and integrity of his country as he is his own personal life, for in the end he has to assume accountability for both.

The subject of group karma has some very interesting aspects which deserve consideration by the individual who is striving to live in accordance with his highest understanding. In everyday life, how little thought is given to the karmic aspects of one's group associations or of professions of which one makes use. Does one ever consider that in belonging to a religion or in availing oneself of the services of the medical profession, as examples, one in partaking to some extent in the collective karma of these groups? In joining a religion, does the devotee ever consider his vicarious association with the intolerance and persecution which have been perpetrated by that sect? Does the person who avails himself of the latest developments in medical practice ever stop to think of the suffering and torture that may have accompanied the development of those techniques? Probably not, but it is something deserving serious thought.

As long as minds and emotions continue to generate hatred, jealousy, envy, and greed, whether as individuals or as members of a group, so long will karmic ties be created and karmic debts be balanced out. When will the wheel stop turning? Who knows? But probably not until all of mankind has reached perfection.

References

[1]*The Mahatma Letters to A. P. Sinnett,* transcribed and compiled by A. T. Barker, 3rd ed., Adyar: Theosophical Publishing House, 1962, p. 347.

[2] Ibid., p. 67.

[3] Annie Besant, *The Ancient Wisdom,* Adyar: Theosophical Publishing House, p. 272.

[4] Barker, op cit., p. 109.

[5] Ibid., p. 147.

[6] Besant, op cit., p. 286.

[7] Barker, op cit., p. 395.

George E. Linton, a retired Civil Engineer, has been a student of Theosophy for over forty years and has been active in the work of The Theosophical Society during most of that time. For a number of years he was on the staff of the International Headquarters at Adyar, Madras, India, where he supervised the construction of a new building for the Adyar Library and Research Centre and served on the Executive Committee of the International Society. He has also served as President of the Portland Branch and of the Northwest Federation of The Theosophical Society in America. He has been a member of the National Board of Directors of The Theosophical Society in America.

14.

THE OTHER FACE OF KARMA

Virginia Hanson

Few people who have given serious thought to the subject of karma would deny that it is one of the most complex, the most profound, and probably the least understood of all the great universal principles expounded in the literature of Theosophy. To attempt to touch upon any of its more subtle aspects may seem presumptuous in the extreme. In particular, as one approaches the subject from a Christian background, one may seem to be inviting an impasse, for sooner or later he is confronted with the juxtaposition of karma as an immutable law and grace with its secret and mysterious dynamics which seem to operate independently of law.

In human affairs, both karma and grace may, in a sense, be said to "happen," that is, they are experienced and experienceable. This seems undeniable fact, so that neither can be denied. We feel instinctively that fact cannot be untruth; at the same time, it can never be the whole of truth. It says, in effect, "I am both hiding and revealing truth." Dare one explore what is hidden beneath what is revealed in the action of karma and grace?

The mere placing of these two words together may seem to be drawing lines for an irresolvable conflict. In the dead-letter, literal interpretation of karma as a mechanical process grinding on and on like a locomotive on a single pair of tracks, there can be no such thing as grace. In the sentimental, wishful, unrealistic view of grace as a favor dispensed by a jealous and erratic God, to be gained by flattery and profession of belief, karma is a concept to be rejected vehemently. Yet in any real and earnest search for truth there can be no conflict, for the searcher does not begin with rejection; he does not begin with any conditioned attitude at all, but only with eyes and mind open to see what he may find.

What is the nature of the reality of karma? What is the nature of the reality of grace? And what is the nature of the relationship between them? Are they two sides of a coin, or are they totally foreign and antagonistic to each other?

H. P. Blavatsky calls karma "the One Law which governs the World of Being."[1] It has been described as the Absolute in the process of manifestation and as manifestation seeking to restore the harmony of the Absolute. It is spoken of an impersonal, inexorable, immutable — but also as modifiable. It has been called a "mathematical equation."

Sir James Jeans, the British scientist, declared that "the universe appears to have been designed by a pure mathematician"[2] and that ". . . the laws which nature obeys are less suggestive of those which a machine obeys in its motion that of those which a musician obeys in writing a fugue, or a poet in composing a sonnet. The motions of electrons and atoms do not resemble those of the parts of a locomotive so much as those of the dancers in a cotillion."[3] In other words, they seem volitional rather than automatic; they are dependable and observable, yet they hold forever the potential of creative innovation. But, mysteriously, the innovation never creates confusion; rather it seems to grow logically out of the inner meaning of the dance. Such steps as are no longer appropriate become transformed into that which is useful to an ever-expanding synthesis.

In his book, *Out of My Later Years,* Albert Einstein comments on the element of unpredictability in atomic behavior and adds: "One need only think of the weather, in which case accurate prediction even for a few days ahead is impossible. Nevertheless, no one doubts that we are confronted with a causal connection.

Occurrences in this domain are beyond the reach of exact prediction because of the variety of factors in operation, not because of any lack of order in nature."[4]

In other words, the creative innovations of nature do not mean breaches of law. They simply mean that the law has so many variables within it that no one can say he has final and conclusive knowledge of all its workings.

So we have a concept of a great mathematician whose nature is law, but with untold reserves of ways in which the law may work out. Even here on our mundane plane of operations, with our limited intellects, it is a commonly known mathematical principle that when we change the relation of the elements within an equation, we change the results. As very simple examples, we can add and get one result; we can subtract, multiply, divide, square a number and carry the process to the nth power; we can extract square root, cube root, and so on; or we may introduce some new element into the equation. In all these ways we get different results. The equation must work out according to mathematical law, but the elements introduced and the relationships in which those elements are arranged determine the nature of the equation itself and what the results will be. It is known also that the solution to any equation, to any mathematical problem, always lies within the problem itself, never outside, although we may find ourselves unable to solve a problem because we are overlooking some element; we are not seeing it whole.

Surely the relationships between the myriad elements of life affect each other and the end results in any situation, in any experience, just as do the elements within a mathematical equation. The law itself makes no exception, but it would be staggeringly brash to say that we know what all the elements are or that we can predict everything that can happen within the operation of the law, particularly since no situation, no experience, is ever exactly duplicated. Although there is but One Law, it has so many facets, so many variables, that it seems to be many laws in operation; and at times we may not even be able to discern law at all because it is operating at a level far beyond our comprehension.

So it would seem that the *mechanical* explanation of karma hardly explains what is taking place. It is particularly inadequate, and holds no key to growth and understanding, if we use it *merely* as an explanation and search no deeper, in ourselves or in nature, for causes — for those elements which will make the problem and whole and thus reveal its true nature.

As karma operates in our own lives, it is undoubtedly the law through which we inherit our own past. But, again, there is a hint of something deeper and more profound. The universe turns as one (which is the root meaning of the word "universe") and we all live in one element. Out of this emerges the principle of relativity. Every part of the universe must therefore be kept, at every moment, in harmony with its own integral balance. This happens, it is suggested, not only at the physical level, but at higher energy levels which are inconceivable to us. We might think of it as a "making perfect" process — or perhaps a more descriptive term would be the invincible divine will to perfection eternally in action. This gets away from the idea of something static and motionless or of something wholly mechanical. Rather it would seem to be perfect rhythm and perfect harmony, or balance, in simultaneity. The will to perfection is conceived of as the Logoic Will, and its operation in maintaining the equilibrium of the universe is, one might say, stretched out in time and space. This might be termed universal or cosmic karma.

As this applies to the individual, it is a mystical energy of inconceivable power which derives from the Logoic Will, is one with it and is — at every moment — in rhythmic balance at the level of the Self. Disturbances (pleasant or unpleasant) take place in the outer circumstances where the fragment, the personality, is focused. The impact of these disturbances is felt — or perhaps a better term is "absorbed" — at the causal level.* But here it does not disturb the integrity and equilibrium because all is immediate and whole; no element is missing, so that everything *is* balanced and perfect at every moment. Perhaps what takes place is a perfectly coordinated operation of centrifugal and centripetal forces at every level of energy. At the mundane level, the action is slowed down so that, to us, it "takes time." It becomes our world experience. At the causal level it is instantaneous.

Events as cause and effect in space and time, then, must be worked out in the personality. And while the personality cannot escape its responsibility, it would seem that the Ego is the primary "mover." One might even go so far as to suggest the possibility that the Ego initiates the events, that is, it uses the law as a tool for its own growth, for it can develop its powers only through learning to deal with circumstances at the outpost of consciousness which we call the personality.

A concept emerging in depth psychology seems to relate to this possibility. Dr. Edward C. Whitmont comments that it has been customary in his profession to assume that traumatic experiences which might be avoided under "ideal"bcircumstances are responsible for the later development of neuroses or psychoses. He suggests that it may be of value to examine this assumption, and he advances the theory that these often unhappy experiences "may perhaps be seen as essential landmarks in the actualization of a pattern of wholeness. They may be understood as the 'suffering of the soul' which is needed to engender present and future psychological advance. . . . In following the development of past events into future consequences, we might discover a meaning beyond mere cause and effect in the way the past comes to view when regarded as the first stage and necessary setting for present and future unfoldment." It may be seen, he says, "not just as accident or misfortune, but as a destined emotional impasse essential for the actualization of our own particular pattern of wholeness."[5]

Drawing a parallel with the development of the action in a drama — using the concept of Greek tragedy as a "mirror of the soul" — Dr. Whitmont points out that the sequence of events on the stage works out as cause and effect, but he adds: ". . . while it is true that the staging of the tragic or joyful situation in act two seems to be caused by the 'right' or 'wrong' action which preceded it in act one, it is equally true that this effect of causation is deliberate or destined. Act one has set the scene and built up its consequences or 'effects' in order to reveal the intent or plot of the drama as it unfolds later in actuality . . . . Although we may understand the play (as) the sequence of cause and effect, unless we are also able to comprehend the dramatic intent or the destined meaning behind the causal sequence, we will not be moved by the inner logic of its timing. . ."[6] He is making the point that there is an "archetypal destiny" for each individual which is known to the Self and that, while cause and effect are necessary to the outworking of this destiny, the real impulse comes from a much deeper level. This is not determinism, nor does it absolve the personality from its responsibility; it does not preclude the concept of free will. It is the "meaning" of the drxma that is destined and must, in some act, be fulfilled. The Ego is indeed the true Actor and the personality is the role through which he deals with the effects of his self-initiated causes. But the Actor *becomes* the role, else it is empty of meaning; it is an extension of himself onto the stage of lifc. The personality may choose whether to accept this fact and thus move toward the fulfillment of the meaning, or whether to delay that fulfillment by refusing to acknowledge the true nature of the drama.

All this carries the clear implication that what happens to us happens by the secret will of our own innermost being. For the Ego is not separate from the Self (using the word in the theosophical sense); it is indeed that aspect of the Self through which action must take place. In the earlier stages of evolution, this is perhaps a feeble and even fumbling process. But as the Ego developes its capacities and becomes more facile in using them, it comes more and more to direct the process and even to pose for itself greater challenges out of the inexhaustible storehouse of past experience.

Thus, we are always in the process of creating our own drama, our own world action, from within. This creation, which in its outer aspect becomes cause and effect in continual adjustment to the interrelation or interaction between the personality and its environment, is what we ordinarily think of as karma. And because, as personalities, we are mostly unaware that, as Egos, we have brought it all about, even the causes seem to impinge on us from the outside. But surely these can no more be outside ourselves than we can be outside our own hearts and minds. The causes are within us, and so long as they remain they must continually create effects.

Once a disturbance has taken place, it may take time for the balance, the harmony, to be achieved in the outer circumstances. We may even have to wait for act three or even later (here for the moment considering acts as successive incarnations) before the event in act one finds its outworking. As personalities we experience sequentially. But to the Self, the concepts of time and space must be irrelevant. "When" the impulse from the Self comes into our lives, then, it seems from our point of view to come in time and space. But what we experience as adjustment in the personality is part of the archetypal "plot", which is already perfect, whole, at the causal level; it has never been anything but perfect and whole.

The Self is not subject to the working out of personal causality because it is not subject to the personality, although, paradoxically — to take some liberty with Dr. Whitmont's hypothesis — the acting-out on the stage and the underlying theme of the drama "are not mutually exclusive but complementary and mutually in need of each other."[7] But the Self *is* harmony, integrity, perfection. Personal karma cannot affect it, however rigidly and inflexibly it may operate in the space-time world of our everyday experience. It has been pointed out that just as the sky's nature remains the same however black the clouds which pass across it, so the Self's purity is undisturbed by the human thoughts, emotions, and passions which move within its projection, the personality — although in some mysterious manner it descends into the depths with us and teaches us the meaning of the heavenly agony. But we have to remember that, even in this, the Self is still experiencing itself when it sees the myriad personal lives through which it manifests. And since it is perfection, it *experiences* only perfection. This is poetically expressed in the words, "Of purer eyes than to behold evil." Unfortunately, such concepts are too subtle for the blundering uses of language. We are constantly faced with the fact that words are indeed, as someone has called them, the broken wreckage of the reality of thought.

Quite tentatively, then, and at the risk of being misunderstood, it might be said that the Self "cares" beyond measure what happens to the personality, but because it is love in the ultimate it is not "concerned." Worry is a vice which belongs exclusively to the personality, in which love is incomplete and which is therefore insecure.

In this view, presumably, everything is "right," and when we see that which we regard as wrong or evil and attempt to remedy it, that is a part of the rightness. In this view, too, life has a kind of "built-in" integrity and immortality. Everything has an inner balance and truth and harmony; everything, in its true nature, reflects that perfect equilibrium at the core of all creation.

It seems possible, then, that this built-in integrity and immortality can be equated with the element of redemption which has received so much emphasis in the Christian religion and without which, perhaps, no resolution of karma is possible. Redemption, in this view, is not to be thought of as coming about through the sacrifice of God in the person of one son, but mystically through the Logoic sacrifice on the cross of matter, redeeming matter (which seems to resist but in reality is ever "seeking" to be redeemed), the process repeated endlessly, down the lowliest cells and atoms of our bodies.

The symbol of the cross is of course a universal one, far antedating the Christian era. We find the conception that at the "beginning of time" — that is, of manifestation — the Logos impressed Itself upon creation in the form of a cross, the pattern of all manifestation, repeated at every level. Therefore the symbol implies, if we look deeply enough, that our efforts are divine efforts unrecognized. Or, perhaps more accurately, the cross is a symbol of the mutual sacrifice of spirit and matter in becoming one. It is not, in its profounder meaning, a symbol of death, even death as sacrifice, but of the union of opposites — God and man in mutual and simultaneous self-surrender. In every kind of cross known there is a point at which the perpendicular and horizontal shafts become indistinguishable — where they are not opposites at all, each being completely "lost" in the other. This point is at the very heart of the cross. It is what makes the symbol a cross and not some other figure. It is what makes the cross a triumph and not a disaster. It is the pattern throughout life, and it is the inner secret of redemption. Because of it, grace is a reality.

Grace, then, is not something that comes "unearned"; rather is the earning something quite different from what we think it is. It is perhaps not earning at all in the sense of achieving some reward as a result of conscious effort. Grace is unpredictable; it cannot be commanded; it operates when it will and as it will and often in ways which may seem strange to us.

In the Biblical story of Joseph, the beloved son who was sold by his jealous brothers into slavery in Egypt, there is a curious statement. It will be recalled that, after his betrayal, Joseph rose from his humble status as a slave to that of the most powerful man in Egypt, second only to Pharoah himself. He was able to interpret Pharoah's dream and to save the country from starvation during the long famine which visited the land. When Joseph's brothers came to Egypt for help, and when he finally made known to them his identity, they were profoundly afraid, for now, they thought, he would revenge himself upon them. But Joseph reassured them and added, "Ye thought evil against me; but God meant it unto good."[8] Thus was grace operating unseen through even a perfidious act. The story of Joseph, whether or not rooted in history, is a marvelous allegory of the universal grace operating in nature and which, we would say, forever makes good come out of evil.

In his book, *The Hero With a Thousand Faces,* Joseph Campbell tells the story of Virachocha, a great divinity of prehistoric Peru: "His tiara is the sun; he grasps the thunderbolt in either hand; and from his eyes descend, in the form of tears, the rains that refresh the life of the valleys of the world . . . The meaning is that the grace that pours into the universe through the sun door is the same as the energy of the bolt that annihilates and is itself indestructible; the delusion-shattering light of the Imperishable is the same as the light that creates."[9] Is this not saying, in effect, that karma and grace, are, in fact, but two aspects of the same law?

Is it not possible that the ultimate resolution of karma is not through an extension of good deeds on the part of man, not even through detachment from the fruits of action, but mysteriously through participation in a sovereign state of being in which attachment is meaningless — a total union of the actor with the power that moves him to action, a total surrender of self and a simultaneous Self-surrender in an act of grace, the sublime and heavenly gift. They mystical energy which is the will to perfection eternally in operation "moves out" into the personality. This comes inevitably like a "visitation from on high." It is experienced within, yet it *seems* to the personality to come from *outside* because the personality has been isolated in its own zone of awareness. In other words, the Christian would say it comes from God — a God who is generally though of as completely outside His creation. It is unexpected; it is unpredictable; and it seems totally undeserved.

This "undeserved" aspect is probably because the full flow of grace comes usually — although not always — when the self has been completely surrendered; it comes to the humble and the contrite heart, repentant and earnestly seeking to be filled with the fire and sweetness of divinity. It is the Kingdom of Heaven which "cometh as a thief in the night." It would seem to be identical with the energy, the active will to perfection, which has been termed karma — the most dynamic, the most potent form that karma can take because it brings about the awareness, in the personality, of its real nature, that total fulfillment represented by the perfect equilibrium at the heart of the cross where God and man become one. The fulfillment is inherent in the very nature of the law itself. For its nature is ever the nature of the cross. When that realization flows into the personality it is known as grace.

Grace has its own purposes, not to be discerned or controlled by man. Not always does it wait for the surrender of the self; it sometimes forces that surrender. When this happens, it can be devastating. Paul, on the road to Damascus, was blinded by it and was three days without sight or the ability to eat or drink. Yet thereafter he preached, through persecution and trial, "Christ in you, the hope of glory."[10]

Paul spoke of being "above the law, in grace," and this is often taken to mean that in some miraculous manner we can escape the working out of the law in our personal lives. Surely one may assume that Paul was speaking of that total union with the Source of the action, that oneness *with* the law which must be dimensionless and timeless. But the individual must some back again and meet his "everyday"; he may even be faced with a particular difficult evolutionary assignment, as was Paul. And again he is subject to the operation of the law in space and time;

again he is on the stage. But there is a difference. The power of grace to alter circumstances is incalculable because it alters the personality, which is the most important element in the circumstances. The theme has come to a climax. Old causes are "blotted out" and new and powerful causes are initiated. New effects become inevitable. This may be thought of as the "forgiveness of sins."

Such forgiveness can hardly mean, however, that the world experience, the life drama of the individual, will immediately become one long sweet song, or that he will never meet the consequences of the things he has done in the past. The drama continues, but now instead of being helplessly caught in its action, the actor is participating in the denouement; he is letting the action flow through him. He meets events with an entirely different consciousness, so that they themselves become something quite different from what they would otherwise have been. It is probably not too much to say that measure of the flow of grace into his life determines the degree of strength and wisdom with which he now meets and deals with experience. "The lamp of knowledge is the perception of truth. The lamp is the passionless heart; its oil is Divine grace; the air that keeps it burning is the breeze of love that blows between man and God; and the boisterous wind from which it is protected is the desire for things perceived by sense of mind."[11] Or, as it was expressed by the 17th century mystic, Brother Lawrence: ". . . our sanctification (does not depend upon *changing* our works, but in doing that for God's sake which we commonly do for our own."[12]

As to what brings about the dynamic moment of fulfillment, that moment when the law becomes self-transformed into an act of grace, who can say? Perhaps it is a decision of the Self, that power behind the action of our individual world drama. If so, we cannot know at the personal level why that decision is taken. Perhaps it is not a "decision" at all in our understanding of the term, for choice is the burden — and the gift — of individual consciousness. Perhaps it is a "happening" that takes place when all the elements of a situation have made it inevitable. Paul Brunton calls it "a descent of the Overself into the underself's zone of awareness . . . the voice of the Overself speaking suddenly out of the cosmic silence with which we are environed." And he adds, "Because the Overself exists in every man, grace too exists potentially in every man."[13]

But I think we can say that the Overself violates no law; rather that when it moves "into the underself's zone of awareness' it is its own fulfillment.

References

1. H. P. Blavatsky, *The Secret Doctrine,* Adyar: Theosophical Publishing House, 1938, 4th ed., vol. 2, p. 359.

2. Sir James Jeans, *The Mysterious Universe,* New York: The Macmillan Co., 1930, p. 140.

3. Ibid., p. 146.

4. Albert Einstein, *Out of My Later Years,* New York: Philosophical Library, Inc., 1950, p. 28.

5. Edward C. Whitmont, M.D., "The Destiny Concept in Psychotherapy," a paper read at Zurich, Switzerland, September 1968, before the Fourth Congress of the International Association for Analytical Psychology, *Spring,* 1969, p. 74.

6. Ibid., pp. 78-9.

7. Ibid., p. 79.

8. Gen. 50:20.

9. Joseph Campbell, *The Hero With a Thousand Faces,* Bollingen Series XVII, New York: Pantheon Books, Inc., pp. 145-6.

10. Col. 1:27.

11. Commentary on verse 11, Chapter X, the *Bhagavad Gita,* tr. M. Chatterji.

12. Herman Nicholas (Brother Lawrence), *The Practice of the Presence of God,* New York: Fleming H. Revell Co., 1895, p. 16.

13. Paul Brunton, *The Wisdom of the Overself,* New York: E. P. Dutton & Co., 1969, pp. 236-7.

Virginia Hanson served on the headquarters staff of The Theosophical Society in America from April of 1962 to September 1975. She was editor of the official journal of that Society, *The American Theosophist,* and Senior Editor for the Theosophical Publishing House, Wheaton. Before her retirement from the United States Government service she was for a number of years Publications Editor in the United States Department of Justice. She is the author of a novel, *A Man Should Rejoice,* and the recent *Masters and Men,* published by TPH Adyar and Wheaton, as well as other works of fiction and of numerous nonfiction articles, including those published in theosopical journals in several countries.

QUEST BOOKS

are published by
The Theosophical Society in America,
a branch of a world organization
dedicated to the promotion of brotherhood and
the encouragement of the study of religion,
philosophy, and science, to the end that man may
better understand himself and his place in
the universe. The Society stands for complete
freedom of individual search and belief.
In the Theosophical Classics Series
well-known occult works are made
available in popular editions.